D0824405

THE
VIRTUAL EVENTS
PLAYBOOK

amplify
imprint of Mascot Books

THE VIRTUAL EVENTS PLAYBOOK:
How to Successfully Train, Facilitate, Lead, and Present
Using the Latest Collaboration Technology

©2021 Lee Deaner, Nick Zerby, and Stanley Saint-Louis. All Rights
Reserved. No part of this publication may be reproduced, stored in a
retrieval system or transmitted in any form by any means electronic,
mechanical, or photocopying, recording or otherwise without the
permission of the author.

For more information, please contact:
Amplify Publishing, an imprint of Mascot Books
620 Herndon Parkway #320
Herndon, VA 20170
info@amplifypublishing.com

CPSIA Code: PRFRE0621A
Library of Congress Control Number: 2021902444
ISBN-13: 978-1-64543-689-8

Printed in Canada

THE
VIRTUAL EVENTS
PLAYBOOK

How to Successfully Train, Facilitate, Lead, and Present Using the Latest Collaboration Technology

Lee Deaner, Nick Zerby, and Stanley Saint-Louis

amplify
an imprint of Mascot Books

CONTENTS

FOREWORD

I would imagine that I'm like many of you that picked up this book. When it comes to office matters, maybe I'm just "old school." I was fully convinced that in order to connect with my professional colleagues, we had to see each other face-to-face. Phone calls, emails, and the occasional virtual conference call were interspersed with these in-person meetings. But those were merely ways to connect until the "real" meetings took place. Now, things are different. That is why this book appeals to me.

The 2020 pandemic forced us further into an uncomfortable era, where many conferences and meetings have become virtual events. This shift brought two questions to mind. The first was masterfully addressed by Deaner: "If we're moving to a more virtual world, how can virtual events be done well?" But, being an organizational psychologist and businessman, I wondered about a second question: If virtual events can be done well, as Lee advocates, then what is their effect on genuine human connection?

First-year human development students learn what any mother could tell you through intuition—a child's growth, well-being, and development are largely dependent upon a connection, nurturing, and bonds with others. These bonds are essential to our well-being.

Healthy relationships promote better mental and physical health. Social relationships are especially important in our early years as neural pathways are shaped by these interactions. But the impact of these social connections doesn't end when the development of neural pathways slows. It extends throughout adulthood.

We have an innate need to belong—to fit in at work, to gather socially as families and groups of friends, and even to pop onto our social media accounts. And, for most of us, the workplace plays a major role in that social connection.

Based on over forty million responses to employee surveys, it is clear that a sense of connection—a sense of belonging to something beyond ourselves—has more impact on one's engagement in work and life than nearly any other factor. Within the walls of the office, connection can take many forms: a connection to the mission of a company, a connection to the purpose of one's work, a connection to the work we do, etc. And that makes sense, as we spend one-third of our day on the job.

The most common form of workplace connection is social connection. Social connection comes from many directions—department meetings, events, one-on-ones with the boss, informal lunches with coworkers, or impromptu watercooler conversations that occur in passing. It follows, then, that the ability to gather in workgroups is essential to building and maintaining that connection. It is essential to engagement.

But what happens when that ability to gather in person is disrupted? When the world was hit by the 2020 pandemic, many of us (I was right there with you!) were forced to explore different modes of connection. Surprisingly, in many cases, the ability to host meetings remotely and virtually proved not only to be as effective as face-to-face events, but often more effective.

I wondered, as did many, what a move to remote events and meetings would do to this sense of connection. To my surprise, results of global employee engagement surveys indicate that the sense of connection with one's team actually increased, rather than decreased, during the COVID-19 pandemic. Did you catch that? In spite of the near-total discontinuation of in-person team meetings, conferences, educational events, and random hallway chatter, we actually feel more connected to our workplace (and the people at the office) than we did when we were meeting face-to-face.

What's the key here? Intentionality. Not only does virtual technology facilitate the ability to hold events more frequently and at a lower cost, it can also assist in making our events more intentional. More leaders are conducting events with an intentional, driving purpose; there is a reason for these events, and fulfilling that purpose becomes a primary objective for the event or meeting.

Good facilitators (managers, trainers, event organizers) are also becoming more aware of the needs of their audiences. They are more skilled at intentionally creating the environment in which participants can choose to engage. Where previous webinars, virtual training sessions, etc. often led participants to feel isolated, alienated, or disconnected (full disclosure: I have to admit, I was able to get through many unopened emails during these ineffective virtual meetings!), today's facilitator has to be more intentional in making a connection with the audience in ways they may not be accustomed to (hint: keep the cameras rolling, as video promotes interaction).

Which brings up the social aspect (one of the reasons some of us value in-person events). Those leaders who are intentional about building a form of connection within these virtual sessions find they can maintain an effective relationship with the audience virtually. However, if participants choose not to engage by turning on their cameras, responding to polls, or asking questions, the connection doesn't happen. You may be better off sending each participant an excruciatingly boring whitepaper, a useless tote bag with a company logo on it, and a couple of (sponsored) stale donuts. Good facilitators set the stage for, and expect, each individual to engage. And where past webinars were exercises in "death-by-PowerPoint," today's successful events take advantage of human connection—seeing each other, interacting, asking questions, and dialoguing as we would in person.

So, what has happened to our sense of connection as we've "taken the virtual plunge?" Interestingly, based on what we find in employee engagement surveys, not only have our meetings become more effective, our workplace engagement has actually increased. One area of significant increase has been that very sense of belonging—the connection to our teams, coworkers, bosses, and the company—that we were worried about abandoning with a remote shift. Yes, even though our last meeting wasn't face-to-face at a five-star resort, we can still feel connected if it's done correctly.

So take advantage of the opportunity to engage—virtually—with the concepts that Deaner articulates so adeptly in this book. You'll find a new world of possibilities when it comes to remote learning, meeting facilitation, communication, and connection.

Because, even virtually, the social neurons are still firing, and we're still connecting.

— *Tracy M. Maylett, Ed.D.*

Tracy Maylett is the CEO of DecisionWise, the most widely recognized employee experience firm in the industry. He is on the faculty of Brigham Young University's Marriott School of Business, and the author of *Engagement MAGIC: Five Keys for Engaging People, Leaders, and Organizations.*

INTRODUCTION

The Importance of Virtual

When we started writing this book, virtual events were (and still are) an effective way to supplement and enhance live encounters. Online events, meetings, and training sessions are not perfect replacements for their live counterparts. At best, virtual events can only *approximate* face-to-face interaction. But as this book shows, they provide unique, substantially cost-saving benefits for both business and learning.

In 2019, many companies and organizations considered virtual events convenient and beneficial—but not mission-critical. All that changed in 2020. The COVID-19 pandemic disrupted every aspect of our lives, especially the ways we work and learn. Stay-at-home mandates created massive unemployment and, for those whose jobs allowed it, forced millions of managers, workers, and learners into an unfamiliar world of virtual events.

Many of us were not prepared to work or learn from home. Teleconferencing, webcam-sharing, and live-streaming certainly were not new, but we had never before needed to rely on virtual tools for practically *everything*. We rapidly discovered—or admitted—our own bad habits and the limitations of our platforms and infrastructure. More importantly, we learned that virtual events do not just happen spontaneously or easily. They require planning, practice, and (above all) patience.

MAKING ADJUSTMENTS

Mercifully, pandemics do not last forever. Strict work-from-home policies are eventually relaxed, and offices and event venues reopen. But the shocking 2020 pandemic will have long-lasting effects. Virtual events will never again be considered optional luxuries. So, to help you and your company or organization prepare for the future, we have adjusted parts of this book to reflect a new business reality.

Chapter 6 covers planning for future crises like the COVID-19 debacle. While it may be tempting to skip ahead to that chapter, we suggest that you do not. There is no shortcut to having a solid virtual event strategy, and certainly no way to undo the past. Instead, we recommend that you peruse the entire book—by yourself or in conjunction with a team—and develop long-term best practices. Virtual events can serve as emergency lifeboats, but they can also be a mainstay for effective business as usual.

While the recent crisis has heightened our awareness of virtual meetings, the economic justifications have not changed. To be effective, any team must have a means of receiving and processing information, developing new ideas (and improving old ones), setting clear goals and assigning accountability, and facilitating every member's work. The trick is to do all this with minimal overhead. Meetings—in-person or virtual—should never consume more time and productivity than they generate.

THE VALUE OF TIME

As a training manager, instructor, facilitator, or other team leader, you have a limited budget for conducting events of any kind. From the simplest office meeting to the most complex event venue, there are only so many dollars to spend. However, the scarcest resource of all is time—truly a finite commodity.

Time spent in a meeting is not a simple calculation of each participant's hourly cost plus the costs of the venue itself. There are many hidden costs to consider.

For example, you must weigh the impact of trainings on employees' *time out of territory*. Is every hour spent in training—and in travelling to and from trainings—worth the cost of being out of action or away from one's post?

There are no perfect trainings, although live events still retain significant value. They are exciting, potentially life-altering, and often improve morale substantially. As great as it is—or can be—virtual, digital learning is not the same as direct, face-to-face interaction. There is no true substitute for the camaraderie and sense of belonging that a live event can provide. So, if you already have a live, non-virtual training program in place, and if it's fulfilling the basics (time, budget, out-of-territory viability) to everyone's satisfaction, then do not replace it, entirely or even partially, with a virtual approach. Later in the book, we'll discuss the virtues of *supplementing* live events with virtual ones, but unless live meetings or trainings are deeply flawed (or prevented by unexpected events), then they should be retained.

For many organizations and situations, live meetings and trainings will continue to be the norm. However, organizations and situations change. If you can imagine a time when live training will be less cost-effective than it is right now, then use this book to up your game—with new information, higher skill levels, greater proficiency and team cohesion—and prepare to make the transition to virtual.

For all its benefits, live training may consume too much of a trainer's or team leader's valuable time. It can also become too costly or take your people out of the game for too long—at a high cost to productivity and profitability.

Participants in live trainings can also forget important facts or lessons shortly after the event. In addition, if your company or organization is growing, then live training that worked for a smaller group may no longer be practical. Even when live training is going well, unexpected things can happen.

SWINE FLU BLUES

The 2020 COVID-19 pandemic accelerated our collective sense of urgency over adopting virtual event technology; a similar event began my own journey over a decade ago.

One of my co-authors and I were gainfully employed as training professionals at a major pharmaceutical firm. Our job was to equip a national sales force with the product information, insights, and techniques they needed to be successful.

Our live trainings, supplemented with remote teleconferences, produced some exceptionally good results. But in 2009, the H1N1 "swine flu" outbreak changed everything. As a precaution, the company banned all non-essential travel. Training fell into that category, but we were only five days away from a

 THE **VIRTUAL EVENTS PLAYBOOK**

training session for forty new sales reps! Not knowing when the travel ban would be lifted, we scrambled to find an alternative. Using existing tools, we managed to hold the training virtually. We met the expectations of our new reps—and our boss—and helped each participant enter the field better prepared to succeed!

However, after a few well-earned sighs of relief, we began to see the unrealized potential of online tools and platforms. We needed to change our thinking—to go beyond just creating a virtual venue. There had to be a way not only to make virtual events more engaging, but also to choose and change the platform to better meet the objectives of training.

In the ensuing ten years, our obsession has been finding ways to fill these gaps—to realize the full potential of these amazing training tools.

Our experience in 2009 was a dress rehearsal for business in the post-pandemic environment of the 2020s. Back then, travel restrictions were not government-mandated. Participants who could be physically present at the events generally chose to be—something not possible during a complete shutdown. Also, the technology for virtual events was relatively limited compared to today.

After the swine flu scare was over, traditional live events resumed, but the interest in virtual events—at least as a supplement—increased to the point where my colleague and I formed a new business. But the implications of the COVID-19 pandemic will be different: moving forward, live events will continue, but virtual will become the new normal.

Virtual, internet-based learning is a high-potential training approach, but it's not a panacea. It's also not a one-size-fits-all solution to the problem of knowledge transfer and skills reinforcement. Depending on group size, learning objectives, and many other factors, there is a wide range of best practices to follow and pitfalls to avoid. This book will be your roadmap for effective virtual learning.

THE BIG QUESTION

The classic dilemma for any business is to attain an objective in the shortest possible time, at the lowest possible cost, and with the best possible results. Or, as the saying goes, "You can have it fast, cheap, or good. Pick two." Virtual learning poses a similar dilemma:

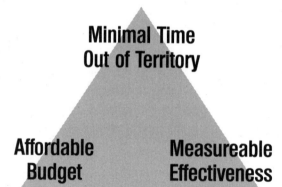

The appeal of virtual is its potential to equip team members *without* taking them out of the action. This is especially true for sales-focused teams, but it applies to every group that must be in the right place at the right time. Training must also be affordable and, most important, it must actually increase practical knowledge and effectiveness. Just because training occurs online does not guarantee it will meet all these requirements.

THE **VIRTUAL EVENTS PLAYBOOK**

This book details ways to plan and—more important—*sequence* the steps of a virtual meeting or learning program in order to achieve all three benefits. It also counters the myth that all online tools must be used all the time, no matter what the situation. Just because a developer added a nifty feature does not mean it will create an effective training experience. Sometimes, it's better just to be human and focus on the people and how they interact, not just the technology.

HOW TO USE THIS BOOK

In many ways, this is just an ordinary book, which is good news because you already know how books work; there's no extra training required. But we have also added a companion feature that we believe magnifies the book's effectiveness.

At the end of each chapter, you will see a familiar image: a QR Code. An ordinary URL is also present for readers using ordinary computers and/or those who dislike QR Codes. Scan the barcode with any free 2D barcode reader app.* Each resulting Web destination contains "active content," including supplemental videos as well as convenient data tables, worksheets, and other tools to improve your virtual meeting and training initiatives. These will be updated on a regular basis, especially as platforms and other technologies change.

LEARNING HOW TO LEARN

From the earliest days of human existence, we have survived and even thrived because of our ability to work together, show each

---

* *TIP:* Apple's latest version of iOS now lets you scan QR Codes directly from the Camera app in newer iPhones. Many Android devices let you do the same, without downloading a separate QR Code reader app.

other new things, and help each other master vital skills. Today, most of us do not need to teach our children how to throw a spear, but the basic principles are still the same. We convey new information. We demonstrate and explain. We encourage and cajole. We require practice and discipline. And we seek feed-back—for our own sake as well as theirs.

Virtual training has not changed the basics of how we meet, collaborate, and learn. It has only altered the environment in which these interactions occur. It lets us overcome limitations of time and distance. It is compatible with our everyday work tools (e.g., laptops, smartphones, and productivity software). Most importantly, virtual events put a human face to every voice, restoring our ability to interact non-verbally, not just through sounds or written text.

However, all that potential will not be realized just because we have webcams and faster internet connections. There are still many ways to fail at virtual training—especially if we focus only on the tools. This book will help you focus on training fundamentals, and how to best apply these new tools to an age-old challenge.

CHAPTER ONE

Planning for Success

Technology affects how people convey knowledge. It always has. Prehistoric societies used visual aids, like the Lascaux Cave paintings, to tell stories and make plans for the future. Writing itself was a revolutionary technology for communicating ideas across barriers of time and space—the core idea behind "distance learning." The invention of paper and printing (in China) and the perfection of moveable type (by Gutenberg) multiplied the dissemination of images and words on paper, making it ever easier to teach others remotely.

No matter what technology offers, the value of live interaction between instructor and learner is paramount—as it always will be. Personal, human connection is the basis of all knowledge transfer, but technology changes the context. At first, technology tends to create chaos, but it eventually results in a more effective connection. Each new breakthrough in communication disrupts the *status quo* of instruction and, once assimilated, adds to the instructor's arsenal.

This disruptive effect accelerated sharply in the 20th century with the rise of digital computer technology. Much of it happened in our lifetimes. The Internet (beginning around 1965) and the World Wide Web (1989) had a huge impact. Online video emerged "only yesterday"—between 1995 and 2004. These technologies evolve so rapidly that we do not yet fully realize their full potential for effective knowledge transfer. As with writing and printing, digital tools like video will eventually become perfectly normal.

THE VIRTUAL MYTH

On hearing the word *virtual*, many imagine something quite fantastic. The hologram of Princess Leia in *Star Wars* or a present-day NASA mission simulator may come to mind. The popular term *virtual reality* also conjures an immersive digital experience aided by special goggles, gloves, suits, and 3D digital simulations. This all makes virtual seem extremely cutting-edge, and certainly too expensive for most people.

But the fact is that virtual communication is not new.

All communication technology has a virtual component. The creator of a written note, a book, a radio or TV broadcast, a phone call, or an online event is not physically present when the recipient reads, hears, or sees the message. An instructor's virtual presence is in the mind of the learner, aided (or hindered) by the medium used. Outside the live classroom or meeting room, *all* interaction and learning are virtual.

Someday, virtual training and events may include the 3D simulations of today's science fiction. But for now, the virtual media for conveying knowledge is quite ordinary. It is a mix of non-digital things (like the book you're reading) combined with the audio, video, and live interactions made possible by the internet—and made audible and visible by the Web and its many devices.

By taking the unknown, mysterious elements out of the word *virtual*, the aspiring trainer or team leader can begin to build a practical and effective knowledge transfer strategy.

CONTENT IS KING

No matter what the medium—physical or virtual—a meeting or a training is only as good as its content. The basic *facts* must be accurate, current, and compellingly relevant. They must also be concise enough to be absorbed by the audience yet also detailed enough to build upon afterwards. The *presentation*, in both style and substance, must also be engaging and suited to the audience.

Finally, as Marshall McLuhan famously said, the *medium* itself is the message. For good or ill, every medium determines the nature and quality of the content. Books and blackboards create one kind of message. PowerPoints and boardrooms create another. Teleconferences and webcams still another. The content and the user experience can be very good, very bad, or something in between. The only difference between these different environments is our familiarity level—and our ability to use them.

Any training and learning medium must facilitate imagination and spontaneous interaction without itself becoming a distraction. Even if the *facts* are accurate and current and the *presentation* employs the right style for the intended audience, a flaw in the medium's design or execution can be fatal. Think of a book, a PowerPoint deck, or a training video that included extensive extraneous material or failed to deliver results. The chances are high that the failure did not come from the facts or the presentation but from poor planning or misuse of the chosen medium.

The best practices for planning and executing a traditional content medium, like PowerPoint, are well established, even though people violate them every day. However, for newer media—especially virtual information sessions, meetings, and trainings—the rules are less well known. Avoidable mistakes happen simply because the tools are so new. Planning and executing content for these novel media is a challenge that can be met—even by mere mortals.

TIMING AND THE TECHNOLOGY CURVE

The time to adopt a revolutionary technology is almost never the moment it first arises. The idea of *videotelephony*, first imagined in the 1870s, had several dubious beginnings as a medium of communication—much less as a platform for training and meetings. Early attempts, like the AT&T Picturephone, failed for many reasons, including poor picture quality, a lack of effective data compression, and extremely limited transmission bandwidth.

The first good sign for virtual trainings appeared in the 1980s and 1990s, with the emergence of proprietary video-conferencing systems. These were usually expensive affairs used by large, multinational companies. They were not applicable to team members in the field—or anywhere outside a branch office. Only with the mobile and webcam technologies of the mid-2000s did the medium become practical for two-way voice and video interaction. However, in the beginning of the "mobile age," there were still plenty of good reasons to wait.

For example, in 2003, Skype Technologies released its commercial Voice over Internet Protocol (VoIP) software service, adding a videotelephony feature in 2005. Many immediately saw this as a means of holding meetings online—while avoiding long distance phone charges. However, large companies and training providers had good reasons to hesitate. The software itself was more like the AT&T Picturephone of the 1970s than a virtual meeting or training room. Mobile devices had limited camera and display capabilities. Mobile networks were slow, often expensive, and inconsistent in different parts of the world. The notion of meeting virtually had captured our imaginations, but in the late 2000s, the tools and infrastructure were simply not ready.

Today, these capabilities have advanced to the point where virtual meetings and trainings are truly practical. Compared with only four or five years ago, network speeds, platform and device capabilities, and the level of professional acceptance have reached the right point for widespread adoption. Meeting and learning virtually has become mainstream for most companies and organizations. The challenge now is doing so effectively.

THE IMPORTANT QUESTIONS

Making the decision to hold a virtual event instead of a live one is a straightforward cost-justification process. Although live interactions are inherently superior, they have many unsupportable costs for all but the smallest, single-location organizations. As outlined in the Introduction, live events have not only fixed costs (e.g., facilities, presenters, travel) but also enormous hidden costs of participants' time out of their work territory. If the costs of live events are prohibitive, then the only viable option is to go virtual.

However, before diving into the technical details, any move to use virtual events must begin with an actual *plan*. The important questions to answer are:

- ■ ***What is the primary objective?*** – Whether the event is informational, collaborative, or training-focused, a clear, measurable outcome must be specified, including the topic or curriculum and expectations of the audience.

- ■ ***What is the most appropriate platform for the event?*** – Not all virtual tools are of equal value for every type of event. Some platforms, like Skype for Business or WebEx, are suited for information sessions or meetings, but have limitations that hamper training sessions. Other platforms, like Zoom or Adobe Connect, offer tools and capabilities that give trainers and breakout session leaders greater flexibility and interactivity. Platform choice is a constantly changing scenario, of course, so the online companion to this book will include a current "state of the platforms" overview.

- ■ ***How can we measure success?*** – This must at least include capturing and evaluating feedback received during the event but must also include changes in member performance.

As later chapters explore, the type of training or knowledge involved, and the specific objectives and performance results expected will dictate what approach and toolset is best. For example, if the need is simply to distribute information about a product or service, then a well-constructed information session (Chapter 2) is best. If more member interaction is required, the meeting format (Chapter 3) is best. If the need is to enhance the audience members' performance in some way, then a virtual training or workshop format (Chapter 4) is the right choice. Virtual is not a one-size-fits-all approach to communication.

The plan must also include all aspects of the event's content—from spoken and displayed words to graphics and interactive media. Each of these elements, plus the presentation time, involves a cost that must be accounted for.

Increased knowledge and skill levels are the most obvious justification for training of any kind, although they are difficult to quantify. However, if training's most basic justification is accepted, then the cost issues revolve around how *virtual* training is better for the bottom line.

Not all the cost differences between live and virtual training are obvious. When virtual training first became feasible, proponents were quick to point out its immediate, top line savings but sometimes ignored the greater, often hidden cost factors.

In a 2014 *Forbes* article, "How Much Does Sales Training Cost?", sales consultant Ian Altman noted that the fixed costs of a two-day, live sales training for a group of twenty-five participants would easily reach $100,000—not including the cost of hiring a facilitator. He goes on to suggest ways to justify such a cost, based on the metric of increased sales per rep.

What Altman failed to note were the unseen costs of live events. When participants—especially those engaged in sales—take time to attend a live training, they are by definition not in the field making money. For sales-related personnel, this "Time out of Territory" (TOT) has a significant *sales opportunity cost*. Depending on a number of variables, that cost can range from hundreds of thousands to millions of dollars per live event. Outside the realm of sales training, there are different opportunity costs resulting from trainees being away from their posts, but the problem is the same.

While virtual training does not eliminate all direct or opportunity costs, it does substantially lower them—particularly the TOT burden of live events. However, virtual events can only do so when properly planned and implemented.

Creating a virtual training plan—including both objectives and costs—is not a trivial exercise, nor will it be the same for everyone. The online checklists associated with this chapter provide some guidance in preparing these events effectively.

TWO TYPES OF ENGAGEMENT

Few words in modern business parlance are more abused and clichéd than *engagement*. However, the word is still a useful way to describe the connection necessary to advance an idea or a decision-making process.

For virtual events, there are two basic ways that participants can connect and communicate in non-verbal ways. Both are meaningful and can assist both the facilitator and the participants. Both can also be misused.

Community Engagement for virtual events is specific to the tools offered on different platforms. Emoticons (indicating approval, disapproval, uncertainty, etc.) and the "raise hand" symbol are examples—comparable to applause and other non-verbal signals in a live meeting. Another example is the text chat feature that allows participants to send messages, whether anonymous, directed, or open to the group (although this can create distractions). Quizzes or polls, shared whiteboards, and other platform tools are also used to create engagement.

As mentioned elsewhere, community engagement platform tools are not always appropriate in all situations. Simply because a platform provides a tool is not in itself a reason to use it. Community engagement techniques that may be appropriate in larger information sessions would be counterproductive or worse in a virtual meeting or training.

The ultimate goal for a presenter when using community engagement techniques is to interact with *all* the participants in a short period of time. The techniques help them understand who is still on, if they are engaged, and—depending on the tool used—if they understand the content.

Individual Engagement is the same basic concept for virtual events as it is for live ones: face-to-face contact and the ability to "read" the non-verbal signals of other members as well as see and hear them speak. Of course, the use of one-way or two-way video alters the dynamic, but the basic principles are the same. Even at different ends of a sometime tenuous video connection, participants can be aware of the other's appearance, environment, and expressions—or lack thereof. (They should also be conscious of their own, which is a given during live events but somehow neglected in the anonymous online world.)

Individual engagement is not limited to smaller groups or even the use of cameras. During larger events, where two-way camera use is impractical, individual engagement can occur as voice-only interaction between two people—typically the presenter in a conversation with someone asking a question or otherwise called upon.

Although visual cues are important to individual engagement, verbal ones should never be ignored. Clear, open, and concise habits of speaking and attention to the habit of active listening are as important in virtual events as they are in live ones.

ROLES AND RESPONSIBILITIES

The most important aspect of virtual training and events is not the *technology* (which seemingly changes by the hour), but the *people* who implement it. The required roles and responsibilities of these people mirror what they are without virtual technology. However, the *limitations* of virtual—especially the absence of live, personal connection—make it important to better understand these roles.

Host – As with live events, the host of a virtual event is its most visible face. It can be a single person or a team, depending on the scope and purpose of the event. A successful virtual event host has the event's purpose clearly in mind and is skilled in helping audience members achieve that goal.

Besides having a mastery of an event's subject matter and purpose, a good host must also know how to connect with and engage audience members. In a live event, good leaders do so by supplementing their voice with gestures, eye contact, sounds of audience responses, and other, subtle, non-verbal cues. Much of this can be accomplished in a virtual, video-based environment. However, because it is more challenging to "read the room" in a virtual setting, hosts may need to re-learn some of the ways to establish an intimate, subconscious connection.

The role and requirements of a virtual event host vary depending on the type of event. Here are four examples of the host role in an event:

A *Facilitator* is usually the team leader of smaller groups of fifteen or fewer members. He or she aims to get each team member to *participate*, whether it's questioning presented information, contributing to a discussion, or practicing reinforcement exercises. Virtual facilitation requires good people skills, presence, and attention to others' words and actions.

A skilled *Moderator* serves a broader, more diplomatic role than other host types. His or her primary mission is to manage member responses for groups of fifteen to thirty participants, while simultaneously promoting the primary purpose of the event. Whether using *Robert's Rules of Order* or a less formal structure, a moderator must allow participants to champion ideas without derailing the original goals.

A *Presenter* is typically involved in larger information sessions or meetings with over thirty participants. He or she should be able to organize and prioritize the session's content efficiently—well before the event is held.* Ideally, and to maintain interest and relevance, the presenter should have the right subject matter expertise. Having more than one presenter or subject matter expert (SME) is typical of larger virtual events.

A *Trainer* combines attributes of the other three types and applies those skills to the task of teaching a specific skill and enabling participants to practice and perfect it.

Producer – While it is preferable for hosts to be comfortable with virtual event technology, his or her success is ultimately connected to their working relationship with a technical producer, a role at the heart of any virtual event. A producer is the behind-the-scenes manager

---

* This does *not* mean creating voluminous and detailed PowerPoint slides, as will be discussed in Chapter 2.

of the event from the initial planning stage to platform-specific chores (e.g., file uploading, formatting, managing invitations and logins) to activities occurring during the event itself. A producer typically screens incoming questions, oversees various tools (e.g., polls and quiz questions), and of course provides support for the inevitable technical glitches.

It is possible for an event host to assume some of the producer's responsibilities, especially for smaller events. However, this becomes impractical as the event size and complexity increases. In fact, a large, complex event may require more than one producer.

BASIC TERMINOLOGY

Besides the roles required in virtual events, there are also technical and logistical requirements:

Networks – There are three major types of internet connections that make virtual events possible, each with its own benefits and drawbacks.

Hardwired Ethernet connections are the most reliable but are limited to buildings and homes that have installed them, thus excluding mobile device users.

Wi-Fi connections—especially the newer generation Wi-Fi 5 and Wi-Fi 6 protocols*—have far fewer limitations for mobile users, but still require an investment at each access point. Many free, public Wi-Fi networks provide little or no security.

---

* For technophiles, those are IEEE 802.11ac and IEEE 802.11ax, respectively.

Digital Cellular Network connections, using 3G, 4G, or 5G protocols, provide the greatest possible flexibility for mobile users, but at a high cost per user. Online video in particular exacts a very high demand on every team member's monthly data plan.

No matter what types of network connection are used, the most formidable challenge facing large-scale, virtual events is the existing IT infrastructure. Most company networks have firewall and other security measures in place, making the installation and testing of new apps problematic. If a system relies entirely on standard browser technology, adoption is easier, but it's not automatic. Existing bandwidth and storage are also key factors, as video files typically create heavy demands on both. Often, a separate, dedicated media line or network is required to handle the traffic—to prevent it from slowing down other, mission-critical IT functions. Coordinating with and securing the support of existing IT management are critical to the success of virtual events.

Platforms – As with every Web-based activity, there are a number of online platforms from which to choose. Some are better suited to one type of event than another; virtually all are continuously being modified and improved (as detailed in the book's active content, which can be accessed at the end of this chapter). In alphabetical order, the commonly used platforms include:

- Adobe Connect
- GlobalMeet
- GoToMeeting
- Microsoft Teams
- Skype for Business
- WebEx
- Zoom

The costs of each platform vary widely, as do the available features, security, and level of technical support. Some require the use of installed apps on each device, which means greater involvement and approval requirements by the company's IT department, while others rely on solely a browser. Nearly all commercial platforms are subscription-based, following the Software-as-a-Service (SaaS) model.

Hardware – Virtual training and events require two types of devices, one for capturing images and sound and another for conveying them to each member of the audience. In the case of a participant's laptop, tablet, or smartphone, the device does both functions. In brief, here are the general hardware parameters to consider:

Video – For the event owner or sponsor, video requirements are relatively high[*] compared to those of participants. For smaller meeting facilitators and group leaders, standard webcams—preferably *HD 720p* (1280x720 pixels)—are sufficient. However, for larger events and presentations, video cameras should be able to capture higher-resolution footage—at least *Full HD 1080p* (1920x1080 pixels) or higher. At high resolutions, video puts a significant burden on the underlying network. However, if handled efficiently, presenter video creates a superior experience for attendees.

For participants, video is wholly dependent on webcams and built-in mobile device cameras. Users' device cameras with *SD 480p* (640x480 pixels) resolution are usually sufficient, although better cameras are becoming

---

[*] This does not mean investing in network broadcast- or Hollywood-level equipment. Virtual training and events should have high production values but should never be put in the same category as TV or movies.

more common.* The basic processing power of user devices is another factor. Older, less powerful laptops, tablets, and smartphones can degrade video performance and lead to a disappointing experience.

Audio – Similar to video, audio requirements for the event owner are greater than for the participant. Microphones, whether wired or wireless, must be able to capture sufficiently high-quality sound. However, for smaller events, a simple room microphone that can capture the speaker's voice, such as a Polycom, works well. Larger events may be better served with a simple lapel microphone, ideally connected to the video camera via a wired or wireless connection.

For virtual events with fewer audience members, a computer's or webcam's built-in microphone may suffice. However, for larger groups, headsets (earphones and a microphone) are essential to reduce ambient noise distractions. Also, keep in mind that the headset should be compatible with the user's phone, since the use of teleconferencing is usually safer than relying on computer audio.

No matter how advanced a user's audio (or video) accessories may be, each user should spend time checking to see that they're working with the event's chosen platform.†

---

* Newer cameras can record HD or even Full HD video. However, if network bandwidth is limited, these devices may need to be "dialed down" to keep things running smoothly.

† The online companion to this book includes a sample "preflight" checklist for virtual event attendees. This greatly reduces the number of delays caused by "I can't hear" complaints during the event.

Editing – Virtual training and events that occur simultaneously, in real time, are referred to as *synchronous*. No editing of video or sound is needed. However, for many events, prerecorded video is necessary. By definition, recorded video is one-way or *asynchronous*. In this case, the footage usually must be optimized.*

The choice of video editing software is relatively simple. For maximum control but a higher learning curve, the choice is either *Adobe Premiere Pro* (part of the Creative Cloud suite) for Windows or MacOS or *Final Cut Pro* for MacOS only. Simple video editing can be done with other software tools, including *Adobe Photoshop CC*.

Hardware for video editing requires a robust computer, with ample CPU capacity, RAM, and storage, and a monitor large enough to display the software tools and visualize the results.

Environments – Whether using a central broadcast site, remote broadcast sites, or individual participant locations, the environmental requirements are similar. **Lighting** must be ample, approaching daylight conditions as much as possible. Bright light sources (especially windows) should be away from the subject and *never* directly behind him or her—unless you're deliberately going for the "witness protection" look. For presenters, having three separate light sources is usually sufficient to eliminate shadows and produce a high-quality image.

---

* Event owners must exercise caution when it comes to editing. Just because a special effect is possible does not mean it will add measurable value to a training or presentation video.

A major environmental element is the ***background*** of either the presenter or participant. It is the visual context that most helps or hinders the overall message. However, the requirements for presenters and participants are different.

For event presenters, moderators, and facilitators, the background should be as free from distraction as possible. This does not necessarily mean a bare wall, but a simple, uncluttered surface is best. A pleasant-looking screen or curtain may also be used, with whatever color and texture works for the presenter. Obviously, complex patterns and vivid colors should be avoided, if possible.

Furnishings, as such, are at the discretion of the presenter. The use of a podium or desk is governed by the presenter's preference and comfort level. Similarly, if a presenter is prone to using flipcharts to write down concepts, then one should be placed in the camera's field of view.* Regardless of the background used, the presenter should always be given room in the shot to "roam" as he or she sees fit.

For event participants, background requirements are less strict, though still important. A wall in his or her office is perfectly acceptable, so long as it does not include a window or other lighting issue. Participants in virtual events cannot always control visual interruptions, such as coworkers, pets, children, or significant others wandering into the shot. However, they can minimize the unwanted distractions by simply turning around, seeing what the camera sees, and making the necessary adjustments.

Finally, the environment for virtual presenters and attendees must be reasonably free from audio distraction. Broadcast

---

* Whiteboards are problematic for video presentations, as they have reflective surfaces that create glare problems.

sites, where echoes or outside noise can ruin a presentation, have stricter requirements than participant locations, where some noise is inevitable. In the case of participants, the use of headsets curtails a majority of these problems.

PLANNING AND PERFORMANCE

In the Army, I learned an important leadership lesson known as the "7Ps." (In the G-rated version, that stands for "Proper Prior Planning Prevents Pretty-Poor Performance.") To this day, I have found the 7Ps to be a make-or-break reality when it comes to virtual training.

All too often, facilitators don't plan for virtual because they think it's "just" an online PowerPoint presentation, a teleconference, a chat Q&A, or a series of poll questions. When they receive negative feedback, they tend to blame the virtual tools rather than the real culprit—their own failure to prepare an engaging experience. If live events are feasible, they are admittedly preferable to virtual ones. But the same lack of preparation that makes a live event boring has an identical effect in a virtual one.

I learned this the hard way in my "crash course" training experience caused by the 2009 H1N1 travel ban. I assumed the virtual experience would be "just" a shared PowerPoint and a teleconference, supplemented by chat and some poll questions. With breaks, the first session lasted six hours, and my audience was bored to death. We covered the material, but they did not learn as much or as well as they should have.

Fortunately, my boss was adept at pushing me beyond my comfort zone. He insisted that I become more familiar with our platform—Adobe Connect Pro—and use it more effectively in the future. We added video, first of the facilitator and later of the participants, and included breakout session exercises to increase knowledge retention and participant engagement. Despite the inevitable difficulties, given the state of the internet ten years ago, our planning began to increase learning performance.

After that first round of training, we learned how to properly plan and prepare for more engaging virtual sessions. Even the inevitable glitches of virtual events proved to be value lessons. We found that participants can handle having to occasionally log out and log back in again, or the fact that online video may not be crystal clear—so long as they can see and interact with each other. Working *with* these tools, not just passively watching, increases users' engagement, connects them with one other, and increases your chances of achieving the same objectives you had once set for live events.

MASTERING THE TOOLS—NOT LETTING THE TOOLS MASTER YOU

Like conventional, live training, virtual training success cannot be achieved by winging it. The planning process is a complex one, combining traditional content and goal setting with the technical requirements of video and audio media.

As with anything new, the temptation is to be led by what the tools can do, rather than by the actual need. Virtual training and meeting platforms include many appealing features—often the result of valid user requests and testing. Sometimes, these features are good ideas limited by the realities of technology. But the mere existence of a "cool" feature does not mean it should be used in every case—or even at all. When used in moderation, the polling feature available on many virtual meeting platforms can reinforce knowledge and gauge audience engagement. But polls can easily become an unnecessary distraction.

The choice of a particular platform or device may be dictated by the features that make sense for a particular type of virtual event. However, the decision to use it must be based on how it enhances the event and meets the specific business or organizational need.

Above all, do not be limited by the status quo—or by previous experience with online events. Preconceptions about any new or unfamiliar process are generally wrong. As trainers and event leaders master the process, they will discover new ways to enhance the virtual experience and achieve greater success.

■ ■ ■

CHAPTER SUMMARY

All virtual technology—from books and recordings to digital, online video—affects how we convey knowledge to our fellow human beings. It enables us to connect with people and information without sharing physical space. As with anything new and unfamiliar, the secret to today's virtual technology is learning to use it well.

A virtual event is only as good as its content—and the platform best suited to convey it.

A successful virtual event depends in large part on the leadership skills of the host (facilitator, moderator, presenter, or trainer), backed by a qualified technical producer. The larger and more complex the event, the greater the need for the roles of host and producer to be separate yet collaborative.

Virtual events depend on wise decisions regarding infrastructure (the underlying networks), platforms, video and audio technology, and the physical environment of the participants.

Active Content

To help you create the best possible virtual event, we have created a collection of "active content"—online resources that will be updated periodically to keep current with technology advancements. To access this free content, use your mobile device to scan the chapter's QR Code, below, or type in the URL provided.

https://letstrainonline.com/ch1

CHAPTER TWO

Information, Please

E very modern business or organization has a fundamental need to keep its members, partners, and customers well-informed. In the past, when in-person meetings were not possible, this was accomplished by distributing mass quantities of reading material—traditionally in printed form but more recently in the form of electronic documents. However, as teleconferencing and digital communication technology have matured, this need is increasingly met by the most basic type of virtual event—the information session.

Because they are not constrained by a physical room, information sessions can be of almost any size. However, meetings of over thirty to forty participants understandably limited their members' ability to interact. Communication is largely one-way in nature, unlike that of other virtual events. Participants must be given every opportunity to assimilate new information and access it in the future. But the participants' primary role in an information session is not to present their own ideas or feedback. It is to observe, listen, and somehow cue the presenter that they are still engaged.

THE WEBINAR

One particular type of information sessions is the Web-based seminar—a webinar. It runs like other information sessions in many ways, including the technical, logistical, and presentation aspects covered in this chapter. However, it is different in one important aspect: a webinar almost always includes a commercial, marketing, or subscription component. An educational webinar typically charges a fee to support the instructor or institution involved. A "free" webinar, however well-done, is marketed to a list of likely prospects who are subsequently encouraged to engage financially with the presenter organization. Participants are not simply members of a company, organization, or movement; they are current or potential customers.

This does not mean that webinars are bad in themselves. They are simply a revenue-specific type of information sessions.

Information sessions can be conducted on an online meeting platform, such as Adobe Connect or Zoom. However, they can also be *live-streamed*, using a high-end Content Delivery Network (CDN) to broadcast video to a larger group of participants. This allows much higher quality video to be sent to screens of almost any size though live-streaming. But live-streaming also results in greater *latency*—the time interval between when the video and audio were captured and the time when they were experienced on screen.*

---

* Latency exists even in high-end television broadcasting, despite the use of costly transmission technology.

The potential for live-streaming makes information sessions different from other types of virtual events (e.g., meetings and trainings) where latency would severely limit participants' ability to interact. The low-latency of most virtual event platforms may restrict the quality of video used but they also make it possible for presenters and participants to interact in near-real time.

CHALLENGES TO OVERCOME

Whether live or online, information sessions can be done well or poorly. Nearly everyone has experienced the agony of a bad PowerPoint presentation. To sit in a meeting featuring a poorly designed, wordy, or overbuilt slide deck is counterproductive at best. At worst, it is a form of semi-voluntary torture. It is the opposite of what presentation technology was made for: the transmission of vital information.

The advent of virtual information sessions has multiplied the problem. Virtual attendees of a poorly presented meeting can disengage more easily—checking email, working on other matters, or even leaving the room—without the social protocols of a live event to constrain them. If a presentation fails to create focus live, it is surely destined to fail virtually, where the distractions are ten times greater.

Besides the accelerated risk of death-by-PowerPoint, information sessions share the problem of all virtual communication: they can be emotionally empty. Without the non-verbal reinforcement that live meetings can provide, participants' overall negative experience can overwhelm the value of the information received. They may have the latest product information or sales figures, but also are likely to experience miscommunication, misunderstandings, and relational attrition. Rather than engaging with the presenter, participants experience a disconnect that negatively impacts their work.

Most of these hazards can be countered, however. There is no perfect substitute for a well-run live presentation, but virtual technology can be applied in ways that not only convey information but also create better working relationships.

OVERCOMING CAMERA PHOBIA

Virtual event presenters very often have an aversion to being on camera. This is a completely normal reaction, similar to the dislike one has to hearing his or her own recorded voice—or seeing a candid but unflattering photo. Everyone has a mental self-image that is more or less true but tends to be more positive than otherwise. This is especially the case when the person is in a leadership role, where self-confidence is an ingredient of success.

However, a large percentage of information sessions presenters are reluctant to be seen online—even those who are comfortable in front of larger live audiences. This stems partly from the limitations of earlier virtual meeting technology, where poor image quality and unreliable bandwidth made the speaker's appearance seem unprofessional. It is also the result of mentally comparing webcam video with professional broadcasting or entertainment. Although, for many, the greatest barrier is simply the presenter's personal discomfort with the medium.

When information session presenters elect not to be on camera, the default mode is to be present via audio only. Some platforms also provide a space for the speaker's photo or other visual cue, but typically the only visual element is the speaker's presentation. A typical session may have multiple speakers with a moderator or just a single presenter, but without actual video, these virtual events are the equivalent of a conference call with unseen voices.

The hazards of this style are easily measured. Typically, participants who merely listen to voices while looking at online slides (even good ones) pay close attention for only 3 to 3.5 minutes before their minds wander. By contrast, with live-streaming by the presenter(s), the average attention interval is thirty minutes. This still means that a virtual information session must include other elements to maintain rapport with the audience, but the ten-times difference in attention intervals makes that task far easier.

Overcoming camera phobia is not accomplished instantly. As with any new habit, being at ease with live-streaming happens with training and practice.

Besides getting outside coaching, one way to get more comfortable with the camera is to simply use it more often, starting with smaller group meetings. With more frequent webcam use, a potential presenter will be able to fine-tune things like lighting, framing, distance from the camera, background issues, and other video-related details. At the same time, he or she will grow more accustomed to the medium, letting it become less distracting from actual interaction with others.

A very important rule of thumb for presenters dealing with camera issues is to be mindful of their behavior during a live event. Although virtual meeting technology has limitations, the normal rules of behavior still apply. The confidence and demeanor that serve a presenter in a live event will do the same in a virtual event. Audience perceptions—positive or negative—are all about the personality of the speaker, not the medium through which they speak.

IT'S NOT TV

Knowing what an information session is **not** will also help a presenter become more acclimated to the camera—and vastly improve the overall results. Live-streaming is not the same as televised broadcasting or entertainment. Full stop. Since an information session presenter is not a news anchor or a talk show host, they should not try to act like one. Nothing can sabotage an online information event quite like a "canned" attempt to resemble a TV show.

This has very specific impact on presentation style. Broadcasters and public speakers spend years learning how to read from a teleprompter,* to create a better performance, generate better ratings, or garner more votes. Given that information session presenters are not aiming for those things, they should not try to act like they are. Audiences are particularly sensitive to this and will usually resist a speaker who overplays the role or pretends to be something they are not.

That translates to several practical rules of thumb:

- **Looking into the camera lens is highly overrated** as a presenter practice.† Such efforts to "make eye contact" often interfere with the goals of an information session. Over time, presenters will get better at glancing occasionally at

---

* Always keep in mind that high-end teleprompters are extremely specialized technology, well beyond the means of most presenters. Teleprompters are either integrated into studio cameras (where the words scroll in front of the actual camera lens) or positioned at two, 45-degree angles from the speaker (to make it seem like he or she is scanning the audience.) They create the *illusion* of making direct eye contact, but only for those who know how to use them. Better performance, not live engagement, is the reason to use a teleprompter.

† This also applies to hosts or facilitators for smaller meetings and workshop trainings, as will be explored in later chapters.

the camera, usually when making a major point, but the goal is to inform, not to be a TV star.

- *Reading a prepared script verbatim is always a bad idea.* Nothing can put an audience to sleep faster than a prepared recitation—even a well-written one.

- *Reading the text of the slide deck is even worse.* It is one of the leading causes of death-by-PowerPoint—in both live and virtual events.

- *Memorized scripts are not much better.* Leaving aside the difficulty of doing so, presenters who are not professional actors should be free to use note cards or other reminders, but always speak from personal knowledge, not by rote.

- *Rehearsal is a good idea, if done in moderation.* Remember that the object is not a TV performance but an information session. Participants need to receive useful, relevant business information. Their role is not to give a critique of the presenter's stagecraft.

VISUALIZING INFORMATION

One of the signs of a poorly-executed information session, live or virtual, is the frequency of the question, "Can I get a copy of the slide deck?" When the question is asked right away, or even before the event begins, it usually means that audience members are not expecting to be engaged.

Relatively few presentation slide decks are actually read more than once—if at all. This is not only because they tend to be poorly designed and lack organized searchability, or even because of the sheer volume of files stored by individual users.

A static presentation is soon outdated, and its key information readily accessible elsewhere. It is often just a "blob" of information—too big to assimilate and not easy to repurpose.

Some companies have banned or severely limited the use of PowerPoint altogether. The use of organized presentations, however, is often necessary to visualize certain types of information and break up the potential monotony of just using "talking heads," within reason. The practical rules of thumb include:

- **Avoid transitions and builds.** There are seemingly infinite ways to add motion effects to slides in PowerPoint, Keynote, or other presentation software. Unfortunately, most of them call more attention to the effect itself than to the point being made. Besides creating a greater potential for technical failure, fancy transitions and builds create impatience and annoyance for most participants. The rule of thumb is: If a transition goes unnoticed, it might add nominal value; if it is noticed as a special effect, it will distract and annoy the audience each time it's used. Also, if you are using builds to lead up to a key point, then that key point should probably be a separate slide.

- **Shorter is always, always better.** There are several popular formulas for how many bullet points or words per line are ideal. However, there are few absolute rules,* only the ideal of common sense. Concise wording trumps detailed explanation. Legibility—including font size and readability—trumps verbal precision. Keep in mind that slides

---

* A possible exception is entrepreneur Guy Kawasaki's formula for determining the right number of slides in a presentation: take the total number of minutes a speaker is allotted and divide by two.

are always intended to *supplement*, not replace, the live presentation.

- *Never repeat content.* What is visible on a screen should never be a duplicate of what is being said. Data or charts on a screen should always be an *example* of information available from other, more robust sources—not just a repetition of the data. The objective of an event is to show participants how to find and use new information and explain its significance—not to get them to parrot it.

- *Use slides that facilitate the virtual event platform.* If you intend to use poll questions or Q&A features of a platform, then insert a simple slide to indicate that event. It will remind the presenter to stop and let the producer initiate the poll or other event.

Yale professor and visual information guru Edward Tufte offered sage advice that is applicable to presentation design: "Graphical excellence," he said, "is that which gives to the viewer the greatest number of ideas in the shortest amount of time with the least ink in the smallest space." As part of any information sessions, the visual presentation can easily detract from the session's main purpose but, when intelligently designed, can make it more engaging.

THE USE OF MEDIA

By definition, a virtual event involves *synchronous*, live video—either one-way, as in the case of information sessions, or two-way, as in the case of smaller events discussed in later chapters. However, there are many situations that call for *asynchronous* video—recorded footage stored on an online platform or service.

Recorded video is an excellent way to retain audience engagement, so long as it relates to the objectives of the session. As with presentation slides, media elements should always be used sparingly and according to the same basic rules.

First, recorded video should be as free as possible of visual and sound effects, music, and other artifacts that serve only to call attention to themselves. Video used in these events will never be nominated for a Golden Globe award and should never pretend to be more than it is—a useful but quite ordinary adjunct to an information session. As with builds and transitions in Power-Point, recorded video presents additional technical challenges, depending on available bandwidth and latency issues during a teleconference. A producer should always test recorded video files on the intended platform before unleashing them on an audience. However, even if a video is technically suited to the platform, the use of frivolous effects in a video will create the same level of distraction and annoyance as they do in PowerPoint.

Recorded video should also be short and to the point. While a video can be a welcome break in the action, a long one can derail the event's main purpose. Finally, as with presentation slides, recorded video must not simply repeat what the speaker has said or is going to say. If the video illuminates a major point and causes the audience to consider its implications, it serves the event. If it is merely entertaining (or worse), then it is just a waste of valuable time.

Not all media are limited to video, of course. Audio clips, still images, and data visualizations can be equally valuable—or equally destructive, if chosen poorly. Apply the same common-sense rules to all media. Choose media elements if they serve the event; discard them if they only call attention to themselves or to the designer's personal vanity.

IS THIS THING ON?

Perhaps the worst practice afflicting information sessions attendees is the habit of presenters calling attention to technical issues. When a slide fails to load, or a video fails to play—or when any number of other, inevitable technical glitches occur—it is all too common for a presenter to make that issue the focus of the event. In rare cases, such failures are catastrophic, causing the entire event to end prematurely. But very often, a relatively minor glitch is made worse by a presenter dwelling on it and even recounting it later in the event.

The reality is that technical problems are inevitable—and probably always will be. Ideally, a virtual event depends on everything going as expected, over multiple connections and devices, and with platforms and content files combining in unlimited ways. An event with zero problems is an exception, not the rule.

The good news is that audiences rarely see the issues occurring behind the scenes. There may well be chaos of some sort at the broadcast location—usually confined to the producer(s) handling the technical details. The host is often aware of the producer's challenges, but, unless he or she unwisely dwells on them, most participants will remain unaware.

There are exceptions, of course. A single user may have a problem hearing the presentation for reasons unknown to him or her. Since the event is live, the first instinct is to text "can't hear," rather than risk missing more by checking one's sound, device, or connection settings. Such interruptions, while inevitable, threaten the event's success and the user's ability to benefit from it.

The right answer to this problem is twofold. Setting technical expectations and outlining help procedures is important. But the most important safeguard is to have a proactive, knowledge-able producer (or more than one, for larger groups) in atten-dance. A good producer is active not only in managing platform performance, but in anticipating and responding to inevitable technical issues. The larger the group size, the more important it is to have a competent technical producer behind the scenes.

The tendency of presenters to apologize for such problems is natural, but completely counterproductive. If the problem is only obvious to the presenter—as surprisingly many are—then they have created a new, unnecessary distraction. If the problem is more serious, the audience is already aware, and any atten-tion serves only to frustrate rather than comfort the group. Such apologies and complaints from the presenter only convey a lack of confidence in the medium—or worse, that the information is not worth the trouble of using virtual tools.

A far better response is one of confidence in the platform itself, in the technical capabilities of the producer, and in the audience's interest in the topic. When a glitch occurs, the best approach is simply to continue with the presentation. Since most participants probably didn't even notice, a good producer only tells the group when they need to stop or acknowledge a significant issue. At worst, if a problem is not immediately resolv-able, the best response is to announce a short break, or, in very rare cases, a postponement of the event. Taking control of the situation means managing expectations, not focusing others on circumstances beyond their control.

THE SECRET TO SUCCESS

All-Star pitcher Vernon "Lefty" Gomez was famous not only for his prowess on the mound, but also for his sayings off the field. Recounting his career to a reporter, he famously said, "The secret of my success was clean living and a fast outfield."

Success in a virtual meeting can often be attributed to fast thinking and good preparation by someone the participants never see—the producer.

In early 2018, a virtual facilitator for one of our clients was scheduled to conduct an information session covering a sales technique for a relatively small group of employees. Due to heavy snow, she had to conduct the session from her apartment, with only a cellular hotspot as her internet connection.

The session involved extensive screen sharing by her producer while she narrated for the benefit of the team. However, less than a quarter of the way through, her internet connection failed, so she could no longer see what her team was seeing.

No one noticed, thanks to the "fast outfield" (her producer) and good planning. She was speaking via teleconference rather than through the computer audio, so the internet failure had zero impact on her narration. More importantly, on her laptop, she had backup copies of all the visual content being shared and was able to subtly cue the producer when to make transitions. She made no mention of the connection problem and completed the session.

The underlying technology for sharing visual images failed under conditions that are all too common. But none of the participants even suspected that she was "there" only via teleconference for more than seventy-five percent of the time.

USING PLATFORM FEATURES EFFECTIVELY

Most of the major virtual event platforms contain features designed to facilitate better engagement, including polling mechanisms and both public and private chat windows. Some include emoticons (e.g., thumbs up or thumbs down) to show audience reactions at a given moment. Almost all platforms allow the presenter to share his or her screen.

Without a producer, these tools are often too distracting to be useful to an event host or presenter. Even in small groups, their distraction potential undermines the presenter's primary role. However, correctly used, some platform features can increase engagement and knowledge retention over the long term.

Polling Questions can be used in several ways. At the beginning of an event, a multiple-choice question can inform the presenter of the group's existing level of understanding, allowing him or her to adjust the presentation to a limited degree. They can also be used as icebreakers to put the audience more at ease. Polling questions are also useful in helping the audience reinforce what they have just learned.

Like any other feature, polling questions can be overdone and overly distracting. A useful rule of thumb is to plan no more than four or five polling questions in an hour-long event.

If the polling question feature allows text responses in addition to true/false or multiple choice, then it can be used for a vital aspect of an information session: reinforcement. At the close of the event, the question would be for each user to summarize the key takeaway for the session. (This could also be accomplished with the text chat feature.) By allowing three to four minutes for a thoughtful response—whether confidential or public—the question would give individuals the opportunity to internalize the information.

Text Chat is a nearly universal feature on virtual meeting platforms and is perhaps the simplest to explain. However, because texting is so ubiquitous, a certain amount of careful planning is needed to avoid chaos. First, the host/presenter and the producer should agree on the ground rules for who chats with whom. Most platforms allow for private chat between members, but that may create undue distraction. Chat with the producer is essential, not only for technical problems, but also for commentary and questions.

The text chat feature also encourages short responses by multiple audience members during key moments of the event. Similar to the "key takeaway question," this gives the producer periodic feedback to relay to the presenter. (It can also be an "early warning system" for widespread technical problems.)

The *Q&A* process on most virtual platforms is arguably the most important way to engage an audience and facilitate the event. On most platforms, Q&A is simply a moderated version of text chat, though on others, it is a separate tool. Typically funneled through the producer, the most relevant questions are submitted to the presenter at or near the event's conclusion. Although this process is merely a virtual extension of a long-standing practice in live events, it can also be used for a uniquely virtual application. Since it is unlikely all questions can be answered on the spot, they can be curated afterwards to consolidate duplicates and eliminate truly irrelevant ones, then serve as the basis for an event FAQ page. In many cases, such questions can form the basis for future events.

Emoticons are comparable to the "clicker" mechanism in some learning management or online focus group systems. Some platforms even aggregate these responses on the attendee list to show how people are responding. By combining and tracking approval and disapproval trends, these systems can provide live feedback on a topic. Analyzing such trends in real time is a challenge that should be handled by a producer.

Platform features should never be used simply for their own sake. However, when used in context and with planning, they can help the participants acquire and retain much more of the presented information.

Screen Sharing was originally intended for the presenter to show a presentation deck to an audience. Today, it is the producer rather than the presenter who is more likely handling the presentation slides—along with live video and recorded media. Screen sharing by the presenter is still an option, however, when the need arises to display a live process occurring on the presenter's computer.

SHOW ME, DON'T JUST TELL ME

Online information sessions share an important similarity to their live counterparts. If the presenter is simply reciting or displaying facts and figures, the audience is likely to disengage. To avoid the potential for a *Ferris Bueller* moment,* presenters must develop their skills when using video-based virtual platform:

Use the Stage. An information session is not a Broadway play, but a certain level of public speaking prowess will keep the event from becoming a dull recitation. A presenter should use video in the way that best suits his or her personal style and body language. If roaming the stage is apropos, then video cameras should be set up to accommodate that. If an office or living room setting is a natural fit, then strive for that environment. If the podium-and-screen mode is where a presenter shines, then

---

* Just recall the actor Ben Stein's infamous line, "Anyone? Anyone?"

use that. The only wrong approach is to force a presenter into an uncomfortable mode of presenting.

Create a Rhythm. Information sessions are, by definition, filled with important facts for the audience to learn and internalize. However, as with live events, a virtual presenter must learn to "mix it up," interspersing monologue, information visuals, and discussion to keep the audience fully engaged. On a virtual platform, the interactive options are actually greater than for live events, but they should be employed with caution.

For virtual information sessions, shift the participants' view every two to five minutes. In some cases that shift could be to a new slide, but more often it should be from the slides to the speaker, to different view of the speaker,* or to a recorded media clip. The transitions should not be too sudden, random, or out of context. However, frequent changes of scene will retain the audience's attention and increase the likelihood that they will retain the information.

Read the Audience. In a virtual information session—particularly a large one—it is impractical to utilize their webcams and microphones to capture their reaction. (Personal interactivity is a factor in smaller meeting and trainings, as discussed in Chapters 3 and 4.) However, most platforms provide social interaction tools, such as emoticons, which can be used to gauge the overall audience response.†

Bring in Other Speakers. When appropriate, additional speakers can be crucial to the engagement level of virtual information sessions. One advantage of using online event platforms

---

* This requires the use of more than one camera—and a producer who knows how to switch them efficiently.

† As discussed earlier, the producer, not the presenter, is the best person to implement these.

is the ability to include subject matter experts who are not in the same location as the presenter.

Plant (and Prepare) an Audience Member. For the Q&A portion of an event, it is common practice to ask others to submit "seed questions" ahead of time, which the producer will include along with questions texted during the presentation. However, it is also possible to ask the same person(s) to be prepared to go on camera during the Q&A. In addition to their question or comment, the fact that the person is on camera heightens the audience's interest and possibly motivates others to participate more fully.

Some care must be exercised when asking audience members to make an appearance at an information session. The producer must exercise discretion in screening requests to guard against inappropriate or distracting visual backgrounds—and of course the tendency of some participants to hijack the session. This "seeding" technique works well in training or workshop events, as discussed later in the book, but can be used—with caution—in larger events.

CONCLUSIONS

An information session—including its webinar variant—can have enormous benefits for companies and organizations with large, geographically dispersed membership. Those who conduct these events with confidence and skill, supported by a capable producer, have the potential to improve the knowledge and performance levels of every participant—and contribute greatly to the company's long-term success.

■ ■ ■

CHAPTER SUMMARY

Virtual information sessions, like their live counterparts, are primarily for one-way presentations with some feedback from participants. They can be for groups of any size, but an audience of more than thirty to forty participants will limit the members' ability to interact with the speaker.

A webinar is typically an information session with a commercial, marketing, or subscription component.

In virtual information sessions, presenters should always act naturally, not pretend they are professional TV actors or broadcasters. Whenever possible, they should avoid reading from the presentation slides or distributing copies of the presentation in advance.

When the inevitable technical problems arise, presenters should avoid calling the group's attention to the problem and instead rely on their producers to address it without interrupting the session. If the problem is serious enough to stop everything, the presenter can call for a break or, in extreme cases, a postponement.

Just because a platform has a specific tool or effect is not sufficient reason to use it. Only use a platform's features when they add value to the experience.

Active Content

To access the free, active content resources for this chapter, use your mobile device to scan the chapter's QR Code, below, or type in the URL provided.

https://letstrainonline.com/ch2

CHAPTER THREE
Meetings Managed

The difference between information sessions and virtual meetings is simple. The former is characterized by *one-way video* from the presenter or facilitator to a remote audience. Once the event involves *two-way video* interaction—with each participant on camera or potentially so—the event is a virtual meeting. Considerably more technically demanding, these require the services of a producer, and are limited to no more than thirty participants (ideally, eighteen).*

As covered in Chapter 2, information sessions involve mainly *community* interaction, a combination of features that allow mass responses (e.g., emoticons, chat, polls) supported by most platforms. Meetings add *individual* interaction, via each participant's webcam and audio, which diminish the need for community interaction tools and raise the requirements for using non-verbal cues.

---

* One-way information sessions can be of any size, even just a handful of participants. It is the complexity of interaction, not the group's size, that makes the event a meeting.

A BIT OF HISTORY

Virtual meetings are not new. Since the invention of the telephone in 1876, we have had live conversations with people who are not physically present. The phone-based meeting was first demonstrated to the world at the Panama-Pacific International Exposition in 1915.* As telephony became more sophisticated, the idea of meeting over the phone in groups of two or more has become commonplace.

Of course, a call is not the same as a face-to-face conversation—unless the latter happens in complete darkness. Visual cues and information are essential for a complete understanding. Before the advent of the Web, visual information had to be printed or faxed prior to the call. Subtle visual cues were missing entirely. Meeting members had to rely on each other's tone of voice in order to "read the room."

Things began to change with videoconferencing systems. Early versions were proprietary and expensive, requiring professional installation, but they did allow people in one location (typically a conference room) to see and hear people in another. Less costly, Web-based versions emerged after 2005. Increasingly, meeting participants could see each other's faces (and bedrooms or offices), share screens and files, and even hold parallel conversations via chat. While breakthroughs in Web technology made virtual, visual meetings *possible and more affordable*, it did not magically give meeting facilitators and participants the ability to make them *effective*.

---

*   Technically, the first long distance call—between Alexander Graham Bell and Thomas Watson—was not a conference call as we now know it. But the thousands of people on Bell's end of the 4,750-mile line—all listening via speaker—were in fact participants in the world's first virtual meeting.

LATENCY AND RESOLUTION

Adobe Connect and other virtual event platforms have relatively low latency, meaning that there is only a short delay between when a speaker says something and when the listener hears (and sees) what was said. This efficiency comes at a cost in resolution and image quality. HD (1920x1080) video is an exception, and currently performs well, latency-wise, in most situations. Some platforms can automatically shift to lower resolutions when network connections falter. For the vast majority of two-way video used in virtual meetings and workshops, such image quality is perfectly acceptable.

Live-streaming, on the other hand, is capable of sending much higher resolution content, such as 4K (3840x2160) video. As one might expect, however, this quality comes at a high latency cost. Even over a high-bandwidth Content Delivery Network (CDN), delays of thirty seconds or more are common, making live-streaming unsuitable for virtual meetings and trainings,* where immediate, two-way interactivity is required.

UNDERSTANDING THE LIMITATIONS

From 2005 to 2015, severe limitations in technology hampered Web-based videoconferencing. Network bandwidth and speed were ill-equipped to handle the demands of video—as is still the case in many parts of the world. Webcams were a novel

---

* For information sessions, live-streaming can be used, especially if some or most of the audience is viewing the event in a large auditorium.

accessory, not standard equipment. Early virtual event platforms were less capable. Many of those limitations have since been overcome, but virtual meetings are still limited by technology-related issues.

Not all members' technology tools are equal. Even in a tightly controlled organization, "standard" equipment is not uniform. Laptops and tablets may have the capability to capture and render live video. Smartphones are often personally owned and therefore wildly different from one user to another. Webcams may or may not be standard equipment. If they are, they may not all be of the same quality and resolution. Network connection speeds and reliability vary widely. In other words, the larger the group, the more likely the disparity in equipment will create problems that simply do not exist in a live meeting.

Some members will resist technology. Out of bad past experience, habitual resistance to change, or genuine preference for live interaction, some team members simply dislike virtual meeting technology. Such bias—justified or not—impedes the success of any virtual event. Still, this resistance is entirely normal and may change only gradually, and never completely. A good virtual facilitator will understand this resistance, but not allow it to become the focus or derail the event.

Glitches happen. No matter how robust the network, how reliable the platform and hardware, or how capable the operators, Murphy's Law is always in force. There are simply too many variables—technical and behavioral—to make a "perfect" session the norm. However, as discussed in Chapter 2, virtual meeting leaders must always resist the temptation to focus members' attention on the inevitable glitch. Instead, he or she should always rely on a capable producer to handle issues and stay focused on the purpose of the meeting.

THE ELEMENTS OF SUCCESS

A virtual meeting will succeed for the same reason a live one does—individual engagement. Adding *two-way* video to the virtual event makes it possible to follow visual cues and protocols, including body language and facial expression. It also draws attention to the physical space of each participant—not an issue with live meetings in the same room. Although video has altered the nature of the virtual room, human interaction is the same as it has been for millennia.

IT'S A MEETING—NOT A BROADCAST!

Virtual meeting facilitators, like presenters in information sessions, frequently confuse their role with that of a broadcaster or entertainer. They think they should be constantly looking at the camera and "making eye contact" with the audience. Performing for the camera—when combined with most people's natural camera shyness—will make a facilitator behave unnaturally and lead to a lack of actual engagement. Imagine what it would be like if, during a live meeting, the team leader made continual eye contact with only one person in the room.

Depending on the location of the video camera or webcam, the facilitator should only glance at the lens occasionally. This takes practice. The facilitator's primary focus should be on scanning the individual video images of the participants, as one would do in a live meeting. Pay attention if someone is speaking, but simultaneously be aware that others are responding non-verbally. When someone seems curious (or indifferent, or skeptical), the meeting facilitator should respond as he or she would in a live meeting—with respect and usually with a question like, "Bob, you look puzzled. Are we missing something?" As this virtual process becomes more natural, the facilitator can look at the camera more frequently—such as when making a point.

This is *not* to say that facilitators or participants should ignore the details of their on-camera presence. Being dressed appropriately is as important in a virtual meeting as it is in a live one. The positioning of the camera, lighting and sound variables, and the participant's background image are important (and will be covered later in this book). With simple instruction and practice, participants can quickly learn how to avoid the "witness protection look" or the "ghostly forehead look" associated with webcam video. Also, simply by turning around and seeing what the camera sees, participants can make background adjustments—like closing a bathroom door—that will make their presence more professional and less distracting.

Of course, this will never eliminate the occasional video faux pas. Learn to expect disruptions by pets, children, or significant others unwittingly making an entrance. Facilitators and their producers should learn to minimize these simply by turning off a camera when the need arises. It also helps if everyone can maintain a healthy sense of humor.

Individual engagement is partly a native skill and partly a learned one. Good meeting facilitators should already possess some ability to listen and respond to both verbal and non-verbal cues, though they should also seek to improve those skills. The addition of virtual meetings to the methods of interpersonal interaction should not be seen as learning new skills but enhancing and expanding existing ones.

Virtual meetings also benefit from the use of effective process. This varies from group to group, as it does for live meetings. Whether a facilitator follows *Robert's Rules of Order* or something less formal, a commonly understood set of procedures not only keeps a virtual meeting from digressing into chaos, it also gives participants the confidence that their views will be received.

Finally, virtual meetings differ from information sessions in terms of content and preparation. If slide decks are used at all, they should have significantly fewer slides with minimal bullet points per slide. Visual elements are preferable to text wherever possible. When holding a virtual meeting, the facilitator should be prepared to engage with participants every five minutes by soliciting answers or comments and by promoting on-topic discussions.

GENERAL BEST PRACTICES

By definition, virtual meetings involve the individual cameras or webcams for each participant. The ideal virtual meeting size—especially for newer presenters—is fifteen or fewer participants. Larger, sixteen-to-thirty member meetings are possible, but requires that some or even most members to be off camera for portions of the event.[*]

This means managing multiple video connections, often involving individuals who are inexperienced with or even hostile to the technology. In nearly all cases, the meeting facilitator should not assume responsibility for those connections—especially if he or she is not an expert with the platform being used. If a technical producer is not used, then the facilitator should at least designate a trusted assistant in the meeting to oversee the technical details.

---

[*] Virtual meetings of more than thirty people are also possible, but usually require professional production expertise.

One of the very first tasks in a virtual meeting is for everyone to perform a camera check. This should happen early in the meeting in order to set expectations and establish a regular routine.

A meeting-wide camera check begins with the facilitator on camera. Then, at the facilitator's request and with the help of the producer or assistant, each team member should turn on their camera or webcam, adjust the position if necessary, and, in larger groups, turn it off again. At the same time, they can say a word or two to check the sound.

This procedure accomplishes several things. It serves as a roll call, and can even be used to establish a quorum, if needed. It also makes the technology a bit less intimidating for those who fear or dislike it. Most importantly, an early camera check cues the members that they could potentially be called upon to be on camera and speak to the group. This cue increases overall attention levels and make passive participation less likely.

A camera check also heads off potential technical glitches—or at least catches them early in the process. As mentioned previously, the meeting facilitator should never dwell on such problems, but immediately assign them to a producer or assistant and proceed with the meeting.

THE UNINVITED GUEST

There is perhaps nothing more frequent in a virtual meeting than the cameo appearance of a household pet. Dogs and cats photobombing their owner's webcam meetings is practically a category on YouTube. Humor and/or embarrassment aside, such events can actually be constructive—within reason.

One of our clients' regular trainers began using virtual events with some trepidation. She experienced a normal amount of camera shyness and awkwardness in the beginning but was helped from an unexpected source. At the beginning of each virtual session, her cats took an active interest, interrupting the opening introduction and staring into the camera. She was able to remove the uninvited guests and resume the training, but it helped ease tension and adjust to the new environment. It also made the virtual connection more personal. (Other participants' pets made similar, occasional "contributions" as well.)

Besides making virtual events more relaxed and engaging, occasional pet intrusions can also serve as camera checks, especially if they occur early on. Such things cannot be planned, of course, but a savvy event host can use any such interruption as a means of mastering the technology itself.

The danger, as with anything else, is in overindulgence. While a dog's desire for attention may serve to break the ice and make participants feel more human, always remember that a virtual event is not a YouTube channel. Unexpected events can be humorous and diverting, but only if they are genuinely spontaneous. A good facilitator should always be ready to rein in deliberate "performances" and keep the event on track.

During virtual meetings—especially larger ones—it is advisable to have some members' cameras turned off and limit the number of live video screens to the principal speakers or groups. The facilitator and his or her producer need to be creative in bringing people visually into and out of the event. The goal is not only to reduce visual clutter, but also to make sure everyone stays engaged and feels included in the process.

For smaller meetings, members can simply be asked to turn

off their camera when needed. For larger ones, turning off a member's camera can be done by a producer or assistant at the direction of the facilitator. Obviously, this should be done diplomatically, using a phrase like, "Thanks, Jean. I'm going to turn your camera off now, if that's okay." For privacy reasons, most platforms do not allow a producer to turn on a member's camera, so a request is always the best practice—and a reason to do a camera check at the outset.

The view of the facilitator and that of a participant do not need to be the same. Ideally, a facilitator should be able to see all or most of the active feeds in order to read the participants' non-verbal signals. On the other hand, the participant may only need to see the principal speaker(s). Some platforms allow for these differing needs, but as the meeting size and complexity increases, so also does the need for a producer.

A MEETING ROOM WITH A VIEW

Depending on the platform used, a virtual meeting can be displayed in more than one mode to suit the visual needs of the facilitator and the participants. Multiple video windows can exist side-by-side or in different grid variations of four, six, or more video screens. Some platforms even crop and center the subject to better fit the layout. Another approach is similar to the "carousel" layout commonly used in music playing apps, with a row of small participant thumbnails along the bottom and only one or two video windows (featuring the

current speaker) enlarged. Most layouts also allow space for other tools, such as emoticons and chat.

Where multiple layouts are possible, the meeting facilitator should choose the one that enables him or her to see all or most of the participants on a sufficiently large display. While participants can benefit from seeing each other's faces, the inherent size limitations of laptop and tablet screens may dictate a simpler layout with fewer video feeds visible.

Managing multiple levels of display options—including the selective appearance and exclusion of video feeds—requires a competent producer. The meeting facilitator should never assume control of a process that distracts from the meeting's objective.

THE WISE USE OF TOOLS

A virtual meeting relies on the individual engagement made possible by the use of two-way video. However, the use of community engagement tools should not be excluded, provided they are used appropriately. The "raise hand" tool can be useful in keeping order, and a platform's chat feature can be used to submit questions, so long as they do not derail the current topic.

Most platforms provide a polling feature and the use of emoticons. Both are helpful when used properly during information sessions. They provide community engagement in a one-way video context, giving the presenter (via his or her producer) live feedback from the audience. However, in a meeting, these same tools can be an unwanted distraction, since the level of feedback from live, two-way video is potentially much higher. Just because a tool exists is not justification for using it.

For example, some platforms offer a whiteboard feature, which allows the facilitator or presenter to write or sketch ideas as they are discussed. This feature, however "cool" it may be, it has several shortcomings. When shared among participants, the disparity in drawing ability and device capabilities (e.g., pen, mouse, stylus, trackpad, touchscreen) will soon devolve the shared display into visual chaos.

More importantly, features like the whiteboard can be detrimental in other ways—by making the users neglect obvious, low-tech solutions. If a presenter or meeting facilitator is already adept at using flip charts, then the right solution may be simply to point a camera in such a way as to capture the drawing as it is being created.* Meeting facilitators need to keep out of the line of sight, but that is a skill easily learned—and less cumbersome than mastering an online substitute.†

Finally, when considering which tools to use and which ones to deemphasize, consider the perils of over-reliance. Nearly all virtual meeting platforms provide Voice Over Internet Protocol (VOIP) audio. However, VOIP represents a greater likelihood that Murphy's Law will derail the meeting. Instead of VOIP audio, have the participants dial in using a regular phone connection—or at least accustom them to switch immediately to dial-in if the VOIP connection fails. By using the seemingly low-tech alternative, participants will miss less if internet connection drops, and the producer will have one less problem to handle.

---

* Paper flip charts are easy to capture on video, but the alternative—physical whiteboards—usually present a glare problem for video.

† Virtual whiteboards should be used by a single presenter only when the visual subject matter is complex or technical and when a premade slide is not possible.

THE ROLE OF THE PRODUCER

For extremely small virtual meetings, usually up to six participants, a good team leader can handle most of the technical requirements alone. Some platforms are optimized for simple, small group videoconferencing. However, as a meeting's requirements and complexity increase, it is always advisable to bring on a capable producer—or at least a technically astute assistant—to handle the platform and let the facilitator excel at what he or she does best.

Think of the facilitator-producer relationship as that of a pitcher and a catcher in baseball. While one is responsible for delivery, the other provides a steady stream of guidance and contingency thinking. A pitcher can better focus on delivery if the catcher is aware of all the changing variables in the game.

A producer's role can be as complex as the platform and equipment setup require. Typically, the producer provides proactive tech support, anticipates problems and resolves them—preferably behind the scene—as they occur. The most common issue, a participant's inability to hear or see the speaker, can be handled by the producer directly through private chat or text message without involving the facilitator or the rest of the group.

The producer also screens chat questions and helps the facilitator respond efficiently. This need is not as acute in information sessions but is essential for larger meetings. He or she is also responsible for turning cameras off, sometimes to shield participants in unexpected visual predicaments, but more often to keep the meeting focus on the active speakers.

Contrary to popular myth, one person cannot focus on multiple tasks and do them well—or at all. The producer is the virtual equivalent of an executive assistant. They make the meeting flow, give the participants a positive experience, and make the meeting facilitator's job far easier.

TYPES OF VIRTUAL MEETINGS

All virtual meetings are not the same. Some involve brainstorming ideas for a future project or undertaking; others involve demonstrations of a new product or service; others involve status reporting, feedback, and direction for an ongoing effort; still others involve post-event analysis. All involve the sharing of knowledge with the aim of improving the group's performance over time.

Sometimes, a virtual meeting can be heavily weighted toward a presenter conveying critical information. However, if that does not involve on-camera participation and feedback from the group, then such a session is simply a smaller information session, as discussed in Chapter 2. If the event requires separate breakout sessions and "teach-back" presentations, then it is a training, covered in Chapter 4, rather than a meeting.

A brainstorming meeting is arguably the most exciting use of virtual event technology. At its best, creative collaboration provides a path to new ideas in which every team member experiences pride of ownership. However, capable, creative team members are usually busy exercising their gifts individually. Taking them out of the field to inspire each other detracts from their productivity. By using virtual tools, they can be more creative as a group with a lower overall cost.

In a virtual brainstorming meeting, the facilitator must discover ways to address differences in member learning styles and tendencies, as discussed in Chapter 4. Verbal and social learners tend to speak first and often without having their best ideas defined. Logical and introspective (or solitary) learners tend to hold back and carefully consider multiple implications of an idea before they are comfortable speaking their minds. Visual learners prefer pictures and conceptual diagrams but may be frustrated by the platform's capabilities to present their own ideas. Physical or kinesthetic learners are potentially the most prone to frustration, since the medium of virtual events is limited to sight and sound.

Regardless of these differences, a good facilitator can turn a virtual brainstorming session into a remarkable tool for growth. As with the live version, such meetings should always be recorded and, more importantly, summarized for later action. This need not be a high-tech requirement but rather the age-old ability to just take good notes.

A demonstration meeting allows participants to use the screen sharing feature of the platform to demonstrate software-related processes on their computers. This is not limited to the meeting facilitator; participants can also use this capability to show their code, user interface ideas, or other relevant work. Such demonstrations can also be recorded in advance, which may require editing. Demonstrations that are not software-related require a regular camera setup, of course. If the software or process is not ready for a live demonstration, then simple slides or flip charts will suffice.

Participant responses to demos seldom require advanced presentation techniques. Even polls and other community engagement tools are of limited value, unless the meeting is unusually large. For the most part, a robust Q&A session, preferably with the questioner being on camera, is the preferred meeting mechanism.

A status meeting, like brainstorming, involves open discussion and idea sharing. Participants are more likely to have their own slides—which should be kept short and concise. Unlike brainstorming, the agenda for a status meeting is more constrained, but the need for individual engagement is high. With the producer's help, the facilitator or leader must encourage participation from reluctant members and moderate the enthusiasm of the more forward ones. Because of the intimate nature of video, the facilitator must also guard members from unnecessary or embarrassing exposure. If a negative outcome is known, those involved should be confident that their issues are not widely displayed. Fortunately, most platforms provide ample security, and a competent facilitator will make proper use of the information.

An after-action review is like reverse brainstorming. The desired end product is new and innovative ideas, but the source is the success *and* failure of an attempted solution. The participants must be receptive and open to change as well as excited and encouraged by the results. In the virtual version of this type of meeting, the facilitator must rely on the security of the platform as well as the discretion of the participants. Such meetings invariably start with a presentation—preferably concise—but should promptly shift to individual engagement via two-way video.

Learning styles also play an important role in such a meeting. Verbal and social learners are quick to speak (and cast undue credit or blame, if not constrained). Logical, introspective, solitary learners hold back, but are potentially more insightful. Those with other learning styles not conducive to video and audio tend to be frustrated but may have valuable insights.

Preparing for different types of virtual meetings is often similar to doing so for a live version. However, the constraints of two-way video should always guide the facilitator in making preparation decisions that leverage the medium—including the "low-tech" alternatives to complex digital tools.

CONCLUSIONS

From AT&T's Picturephone to the stories of countless science fiction writers, the idea of meeting virtually has captured the public's imagination. Being physically present, while beneficial, is no longer mandatory. The holograms of *Star Wars* are well beyond our reach, but the internet has made virtual connection a mostly satisfactory proxy for face-to-face contact.

With the advancement of two-way video and the platforms that support it, virtual meetings are reality now for most companies and organizations. To implement them, however, the technical issues must be mastered, and the human elements accommodated.

The former has a simple solution: rather than attempt to handle the technical aspects of a virtual meeting alone, a good team leader or facilitator should work with a technical producer. Without that partnership, virtual meetings of any kind will prove disappointing.

The human factors are formidable but solvable. The fact that each user has different devices and skill levels can be addressed with careful planning and management. The fact that some people simply resent the new technology can be met—at least in part—by making the virtual meeting process more normal and by achieving measurable success. While glitches and snafus may be inevitable, focusing on them is not. As facilitators learn *not* to focus on glitches but on the substance of their meetings, they will make the technology more real than its science fiction persona.

In the end, the real secret to virtual meetings is to be more human. Using technology to serve non-technological needs for connection, interaction, and engagement, rather than for its own sake, virtual events will increasingly serve their true purpose.

■ ■ ■

CHAPTER SUMMARY

Virtual meetings are characterized by two-way audio and video interaction between all the members. In contrast, information sessions primarily use one-way video and audio. This limits the number of participants to no more than twenty-five to thirty, with about eighteen constituting the "sweet spot."

Before any meeting, every member should test their camera, microphone, and general lighting conditions. They should also look behind them to make sure the background is free from needless distractions.

For larger meetings, it's wise to have participants keep their webcams off until they are asked to speak or otherwise contribute.

Smaller virtual meetings can be facilitated by a technically astute assistant, but larger ones may require the expertise of a technical producer.

As a general rule, keeping the audio portion of a virtual meeting as a separate, dial-in teleconference (rather than using VOIP) will minimize disruptions caused by slow or inconsistent internet connections.

Active Content

To access the free, active content resources for this chapter, use your mobile device to scan the chapter's QR Code, below, or type in the URL provided.

https://letstrainonline.com/ch3

CHAPTER FOUR

Virtual Training Essentials

n 1885, Hermann Ebbinghaus published his findings on the subject of memory—or more accurately, the lack of it. The "forgetting curve" that bears his name shows how we rapidly lose new information when there is no attempt to retain it. This is partly a survival mechanism. If we remembered 100 percent of every new thing we encountered, our brains would not be able to function for long. However, for important new tasks, our tendency to forget is the principal challenge to all training and learning efforts.

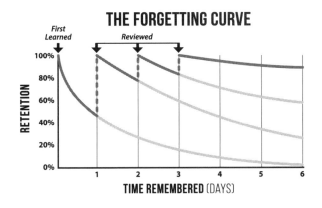

Ebbinghaus theorized that repetition and other techniques would counter our natural forgetfulness. He also researched the concept that eventually became known as the "learning curve," whereby the more a person *experiences* a new task or concept over time, the more permanent their acquired knowledge or skill. Today, it is generally agreed that people retain information to a greater degree by *participating* than passively *receiving* information. We retain even more by *doing* the activity ourselves—preferably with external guidance.

RETENTION OF LEARNING

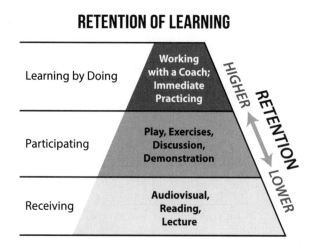

For live training, the traditional elements of receiving information, participation, and practice are well established. They can also be expensive, in terms of immediate training costs and time out of market. The virtual alternative can address these costs, but should only be attempted if it can be done effectively.

THE VIRTUAL CLASSROOM

Virtual trainings or workshops are similar to the virtual meetings discussed in the previous chapter. Unlike information sessions, they both employ two-way video and are therefore more dependent on *individual engagement* (seeing and hearing one another) than on *community engagement* (e.g., emoticons, chat, polls). They therefore place similar demands on the facilitator/instructor and on his or her technical producer. However, trainings are unique in several important ways.

Time. Of the three types of virtual events, training is the least constrained by time limitations. An information session should seldom exceed sixty to ninety minutes and is nearly always self-contained—a one-time event.* Virtual meetings can and often should be conducted more frequently but should never be marathons. Virtual trainings, on the other hand, need to be as long as the subject matter requires. Session length—and breaks—within a training need to be reasonable, of course, but if the knowledge is crucial, then the learning process should not be artificially limited by the clock.

Breakouts. The most significant difference for trainings is the use of breakout sessions. To counter the Ebbinghaus forgetting curve, virtual trainers—like their live event counterparts—must do more than convey information to a passive audience. Even if the material is visually and audibly brilliant, the recipient must have frequent opportunities to discuss, play with, exercise, demonstrate, and even practice the new concept or skill. This can be done in a virtual breakout session where class members

---

* Exceptions to this rule of thumb are frequent but seldom successful. No matter how efficient a virtual information session may be, it should always be used with restraint, and reserved for truly worthwhile topics.

form separate groups to process the material and explore ways to implement it.

Teach-Backs. Another key difference with virtual trainings or workshops is the practice of presenting back to the group. Just like their live event counterparts, this adds a level of reinforcement to the entire learning experience and gives each audience member the opportunity to own and internalize the material.

Each of the distinctions of a virtual training are derived from the live counterpart. However, because the former is happening online, with the inevitable prospect of Murphy's Law asserting itself, both trainers and producers must learn patience—and a new set of skills to augment their own.

LEARNING STYLES

In the previous chapter, we discussed the impact of different learning styles or tendencies on a brainstorming session or other virtual meeting. When using a virtual platform explicitly for learning, it is important to know how—and whether—the current tools and platforms can benefit learners with different abilities and perceptions.

Visual Emphasis: Presentation of images and illustrations—not to mention the live video image of the actual presenter or a prerecorded video or animation—is a natural component of all major virtual event platforms, but must be done in a relevant manner. Presenting flashy visuals for their own sake does nothing to further the learning objective.

Auditory Emphasis: Besides creating a clear, distraction-free audio environment, a good virtual trainer will include narrative story elements to convey the material more effectively. These story elements can be part of the primary training session or used as assignments in breakout groups.

Kinesthetic Emphasis: At first glance, virtual training does not seem to be well adapted to physical learning activities—future AR goggles and gloves notwithstanding. However, the mere inclusion of physical activities, from sufficiently frequent breaks to opportunities to present while standing during teach-backs, can help meet this need.

Reading Emphasis: There is *always* more content available than can be comfortably included in a virtual training session. For those who prefer reading, and for those who don't but need to find information later, an easily accessible and searchable repository of curated material is essential.

In other words, a virtual training can include all four elements, benefitting every individual learning style or preference.

PERSONALITY STYLES

In addition to addressing different learning styles, virtual training sessions must also consider the different personality types and how they impact communication—both as instructors and as learners processing information. Whether the medium is visual, verbal, audible, or text-based (or a combination), how people handle it varies widely:

Drivers: Normally, this type of person is the first to raise a hand or provide answers, which are usually short and concise. They are easily distracted if they feel there are too many details. If chatting answers, they will do so quickly, and their answers are normally less than five words.

Analytical: Normally, Analytical types are the last to raise their hand, with the possible exception of Amiables. When a question is asked, they need to process the question first, formulate the answer, and then volunteer to speak. Normally, you need to wait for a second wave of volunteers of this type. When they answer, be prepared for a longer, more detailed explanation. With chat responses, it will take them longer, and they normally provide longer, more detailed answers. As one would expect, they like detailed slides.

Amiable: Normally, such individuals are slow to raise their hands if they raise them at all. Many times, you need to call on them. Their answers will vary, but be prepared to give them an out, such as phone-a-friend or handing off to someone else, if the answer is not correct because they will go into their shell if they feel like they let people down.

Expressive: These people are very exuberant, will raise their hand, and volunteer before they know the answer—sometimes before they even heard the question—so you may need to repeat it. Answers will turn into discussions with the facilitator. In chat, they may have short to medium length answers, but there will normally be multiple chats to complete. Typically in a group chat setting, they will be in response to other answers. You will need to have a plan to close out the answers/comments with Expressives, because they will continue to have a conversation with you if possible.

It is important to have an idea of the personality styles of your participants. But at the same time, you should utilize multiple mediums within a virtual training session, in order to engage each of the personality styles. Many people actually have a dominant personality style, but also have a secondary style as well. This affects how they interact and engage. For example, my dominant personality style is Analytical, but my secondary is Expressive. In a session, I am one of the later people to raise a hand, but then when it gets to answering the question or making a comment, I am more likely to get into a discussion. At that point, it is good for the facilitator to let me know when it's time to transition to the next item.

In the virtual environment, just like the live environment, you must make sure you are engaging people in multiple ways. Amiables and Expressives like to connect with people, so video and/or pictures are important. Drivers want the key information, so concise, bulleted points on slides or relevant content is important. Analyticals like details, so detailed slides will engage them as well as provide them with potential resources.

Sometimes you may know that your group as a whole has a dominant personality trait. For example, medical science liaisons or engineers are more Analytical, so they may like detailed slides for forty-five minutes to an hour. But if you put an Expressive or Driver into that situation, they will be done in ten minutes. It can become an interesting balancing act.

PLATFORM AND SUPPORT CONSIDERATIONS

When considering a virtual training program, the choice of platform is far more critical than for information sessions. One-way video is not sufficient. A good platform for training must robustly support multiple camera feeds and flexible layouts or camera methodologies, as described below. Most importantly, it must allow separate groups to "gather" virtually for breakout sessions, each with its own secure environment for private discussions.

As of this writing, both Adobe Connect and Zoom Video employ most of the capabilities needed for effective virtual training, although the field is constantly changing. (In the book's active content, the authors will maintain a list of virtual platforms and their current capabilities.) In cases where the training session does not involve breakouts or teach-backs—which would essentially make them virtual meetings—other platforms would meet the need.

One virtual event platform, Adobe Connect, also supports third-party plugins or add-ons. These typically add new functionality or tools to the platform beyond its native capabilities, and can include things like timers, anonymous chat, games, and collaboration tools. However, as with a platform's built-in tools, none of these should be used simply for their own sake or because of a "cool" factor. What may seem like a brilliant tool (such as a whiteboarding extension) may create more distraction and technical challenges than a "low tech" equivalent (namely, pointing a camera at a flipchart).

No matter what platform is used, effective virtual training requires the services of a competent technical producer. From simple setups to complex ones, and for both on-site and off-site broadcast by the trainer, it is simply outside a presenter's scope to handle the myriad details of a training or workshop event with one or more breakout sessions. Even the use of a technically astute and trusted assistant is insufficient to handle the complexity of even a small event.

The producer's role includes camera control (manual or remote), switching camera feeds and layouts, advancing slides and playing media, keeping track of time, curating member questions, monitoring platform performance, and dealing with inevitable technical glitches—behind the scenes—letting the instructor do his or her job well.

With a good producer, the virtual instructor can begin breaking the bad habit of calling attention to the technology when it fails. Making excuses for the inevitable crash or connection problem only distracts from the learning goals and encourages the technology-shy (or technology-hostile) members to disengage.

CAMERA METHODOLOGIES

Virtual training involves as few as four to six (not counting the trainer) to no more than thirty individuals. For technical as well as pedagogic reasons, the size of the group dictates the configuration or layout of multiple video screens—plus whatever tools are in use. Sometimes, these layouts are limited simply by the available screen real estate of a typical laptop or tablet. For larger groups, having every member's video feed on screen as a tiny thumbnail would be of little value.*

The Classroom Approach: For very small groups of six to eight participants, having everyone's video feed visible at once is usually possible. Depending on the platform, and the need to display the necessary tools, the *Brady Bunch* approach can provide everyone with non-verbal cues and a sense of group cohesion.

---

* The only possible exception to this rule might be the instructor. If he or she has a sufficiently large display and support from the platform and related network infrastructure, then an "auditorium" view of the entire class might be warranted—if only to let the instructor gauge non-verbal responses.

This layout is ideal for breakout groups. It also puts a greater onus on the participants to be mindful of their visual environment, background, and appearance.

As with all training methodologies, the platform should allow the trainer or breakout group facilitator—with a producer's help—to switch to a presentation, a media clip, a shared screen, or to a single video feed (such as that of the instructor) when needed. Seeing each other can have positive learning effects, but if attention should be focused on something else, that takes priority.

The Comment/Question Approach: For groups of any size, there should be a layout option for only two or three participants to be visible. This requires a coordinated effort by the trainer and the producer to ask the speaker to turn on their camera, turn off cameras of those not in the conversation, and generally manage the visual conversation.

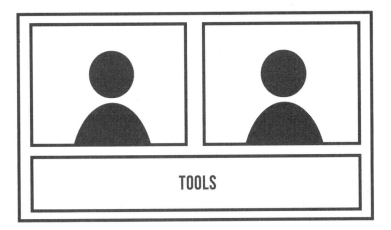

TOOLS

Platform tools, such as emoticons or "raise hand" indicators, may be used with this approach, so long as they do not detract from the educational purpose of the layout—to capture all aspects of a Q&A or other conversational exchange. An alternative to using the "raise hand" mechanism is simply for a participant to turn on his or her camera to indicate they have a question. The producer then controls when that person would be visible—preferably when the facilitator has finished answering the previous question.

As in a live classroom, the virtual trainer or facilitator will finish his or her comment or thought before calling on the next person with a question. When participants are more comfortable with the process, the Q&A session can become a rotation of user cameras that continues until all comments are done—or the facilitator has to stop the session and move on.

The Round Robin Approach: When larger groups are assigned to breakout sessions, they usually report back to the entire group, as will be discussed later. To do this, groups of four to six video feeds, comparable to panel presentations on cable news, are necessary.

Both the trainer and the producer are heavily involved in this approach to make sure all the sub-group members are visible (and audible), to switch to a single screen or presentation when necessary, and to manage time, giving each sub-group their chance to present. Platform tools are less necessary here, since the emphasis is on seeing and hearing the group's findings.

No single camera methodology is mandatory for every situation, but one should use the camera to provide the highest level of face-to-face engagement possible. The purpose of doing so is not to emulate a television show but to become more like a live classroom, where everyone is able to see the facilitator *and* each other. The ultimate goal is to create a visual environment for good learning outcomes over long distances.

SETUP AND PREPARATION

Virtual training and learning events usually start with the presenter's location. The producer can be on-site or off-site, depending on many factors. However, the room/lighting/camera setup, platform configurations, and all network connections should be

THE **VIRTUAL EVENTS PLAYBOOK**

rigorously tested well beforehand. The room itself should not be held to the standards of a high-end studio (since a training is *not* a performance or a broadcast) but it should give the trainer a virtual venue that complements his or her skills.

Regardless of whether or not the producer is physically present, he or she should always use two separate computers for a training: one to manage the platform, including feeds and layouts, and the other—besides being an emergency backup for the first system—to monitor what the class members are experiencing. Very often, time delays and network connection issues cannot be easily detected on the host system (and certainly not by the presenter), so the second system can serve as an early warning system for potential glitches.

Besides checking the technical details beforehand, the trainer or facilitator should always prepare and test all the content thoroughly. Presentation decks should be short and concise— fewer slides, minimal bullet points, and an aversion to transition effects. On-screen time should be employed wherever possible, and screen sharing should be rehearsed. If pre-recorded media clips are required, then testing each media element is essential. No matter how many successful trainings have been done in the past, rehearsals are a requirement.

Finally, when preparing a virtual training, the trainer should always plan to use individual engagement techniques with much greater frequency than is typical for information sessions or even meetings. Whether the interaction is overt (asking a question) or more subtle (responding to a non-verbal cue), involving the learner is critical. *A good rule of thumb is to plan for one engagement every five minutes.* It can either be a community engagement (e.g., emoticon use, a poll, or other platform feature), or an individual engagement involving one or more event participants.

As mentioned previously, a trainer should avoid any undue attention to technical glitches that will invariably occur. A healthy working relationship with a producer goes far to keeping the trainer's focus where it really needs to be.

During the first few minutes of a training, each participant should be asked to turn on his or her camera. Even if it will be turned off immediately—as is the case for larger groups—this practice helps every member be aware of his or her physical environment and be more prepared to participate later on.

THE ANATOMY OF A BREAK

Virtual training, like its live counterpart, takes the time it needs to take. But no matter how long that is, breaks are an absolute necessity. No single segment of a virtual training (or any virtual event, for that matter) should ever be longer than one to one-and-a-half hours. Full stop.

Managing breaks is an art form. People naturally tend to be less focused afterward and often return at different times. Besides being ready to re-immerse the participants in the subject, a trainer can use other methods to reboot the session. In addition to playing music and displaying a countdown clock, the break screen can also include short recaps of concepts taught or teasers of future content. Once everyone has returned, the use of game-like mechanisms or pop quizzes may be appropriate.

BREAKOUT SESSIONS

The hallmark of virtual trainings—as distinguished from meetings—is the breakout session. As a way of reinforcing training content, this is perhaps the best way to overcome the natural tendency to forget and encourage members to internalize and practice the material.

Breakout sessions are simply small meetings held within a larger group meeting. At designated moments in the training, the facilitator—with the producer's assistance—divides the group randomly or by meaningful criteria, such as members of the same sales territory. Each group splits off and then meets—virtually—to discuss a topic, brainstorm about ways to apply it, or conduct an assigned practice exercise. This typically follows the "everybody sees everybody" methodology described above.

During a breakout session, a team leader or facilitator may be chosen, and a note-taker or scribe is usually required. Someone can also serve as timekeeper, although the event producer—with the help of a countdown clock—can also monitor the time.

The activity of a breakout group can be as varied and innovative as imaginations allow. In a sales training, breakout members can come up with and practice elevator pitches for a new product or develop answers to objections. If the training is an extension of previous knowledge, then the group can discuss how the new material will affect their standard procedure. Breakouts are ideal for role-playing and other scenarios where verbal fluency and listening skills are highly valued.

Individual breakout members can take their own notes, of course. However, the role of a note-taker is still essential—to record the group's progress or note any questions for the instructor. If a whiteboard feature is used (or a camera pointed at a flip chart), that material should be recorded for discussion by the larger group. As with virtual events in general, the existence of tools within a platform should not dictate or constrain what the breakout group does, but instead should facilitate behavior similar to that of a live meeting.

TEACH-BACK SESSIONS

One of the most effective ways to convey essential information is to have the learner take ownership of it. Whether a breakout group agrees entirely with a concept, takes strong exception to it, or something in between, the act of presenting back to the larger group cements the information for the long term.

Teach-back presentations can be as varied as the breakout sessions that preceded them. A single spokesman can summarize what the group did, or the entire group can present—or role-play—the key concepts. If the group is prone to competitiveness, then a game component is reasonable, provided the "winning" criteria fits the instructor's overall learning goals.

Presentations during teach-backs should usually be verbal, although visuals can be used in moderation. The driving concern, of course, is time. With a large overall group, the length and scope of each teach-back usually has to be closely monitored.

A key element of the teach-back is a Q&A segment with the larger group. Facilitated by the trainer, fielding new questions on a breakout session is another way to embed the information and help each member internalize it.

SEPARATE AND RE-GROUP

Virtual training sessions, like their live counterparts, have enormous potential to utilize the *differences* in individual learning styles and personality types to achieve optimal results. By utilizing smaller breakout sessions and teach-backs, instructors do not need to force everyone into a single model but can leverage everyone's unique perspectives.

During a recent virtual training series on sales effectiveness, a client planned a session on the topic of handling objections. After covering basic concepts, the group split up into smaller breakout sessions, using Adobe® Connect™ "rooms." Each group used a software module, called a pod, as a virtual flip-chart to record the smaller group's ideas.

The breakout assignment was simple. Each group was given only one sales objection and told to discuss how to handle it. After the breakout sessions concluded, the entire group reconvened and each group presented their findings in a teach-back presentation, using their flipchart as the visual.

Each teach-back presentation was unique, depending on the personality type of the member leading the breakout or recording the findings. Each objection was covered thoroughly, with lively Q&A from the larger group. Because each breakout pursued a single topic as a small group, the strengths of each member carried greater importance. The possibility of repetition, boredom, and indifference was far less than it would have been in a larger group discussion.

Of course, the same results can be accomplished in a live setting. But because the virtual platform (in this case, Adobe Connect) was used wisely, the same learning potential was achieved.

VIRTUAL LEARNING OBJECTIVES
(WITH ACTUAL RESULTS)

Every trainer, no matter what venue he or she uses, develops a plan based on measurable learning objectives. Transferring knowledge has a business value rooted in the productivity of each member of the workforce. Whether that value is top line-related (e.g., higher sales volume) or bottom line-related (e.g., performance efficiency), training must always be based on that reality.

The challenge is to identify the areas of skill and knowledge that will benefit the most from virtual training as opposed to live events. Manual tasks, such as installing or repairing equipment, can have a virtual component, but must still include live, hands-on experience. Physical training for rehabilitation, wellness, or recreation are similarly limited by the need to perform a task or use a specialized piece of equipment. However, *knowledge-centric tasks*, particularly those involving communication skills and verbal fluency, are well suited to a virtual approach. The equipment used to communicate (e.g., PCs, mobile devices, and network connections) are the same for training as they are for work, so the "classroom" already exists.

The list of areas best suited to virtual training includes sales, customer service, technical support, research and development, human resource management business communication software development, counseling, and other fields of human endeavor. Virtual training can also be used effectively as a supplement to training of a more physical nature. A computer repair trainee (or a professional athlete) must have hands-on experience in order to improve his or her core skills and knowledge. However, such a person also needs the vast store of knowledge and performance information that the virtual environment provides.

Virtual training and live training are not mutually exclusive—even in knowledge-centric and verbal fluency realms. When a sales force receives effective virtual training on a new product line, the following live training is far more powerful. Team members will know what questions to ask and be far more prepared to apply their new knowledge in a live event.

Virtual training—like all virtual events—is a significant way to lower costs (especially TOT costs), convey vital information, and improve individual performance. When done properly, it can add to an organization's or company's measurable success.

■ ■ ■

CHAPTER SUMMARY

Virtual trainings should be structured in content-appropriate blocks of time, supplemented with small group breakout sessions and "teach-back" sessions, where trainees can recount the results of their breakout sessions to the larger group.

Presentation slides for virtual trainings should be as short and concise as possible to allow for the greatest possible opportunity for instructor-learner interaction. Detailed summaries and supporting content should always be provided after the training has concluded.

Always limit the duration of each presentation block or session to sixty to ninety minutes, maximum, with adequate breaks between sessions.

Platform-specific engagements, such as emoticons or polls, should be used more frequently during virtual trainings than they are in information sessions or virtual meetings. A frequency of one such engagement every five minutes is optimal, provided the engagement is relevant.

Active Content

To access the free, active content resources for this chapter, use your mobile device to scan the chapter's QR Code, below, or type in the URL provided.

https://letstrainonline.com/ch4

THE **VIRTUAL EVENTS PLAYBOOK**

CHAPTER FIVE

Delivering Results

n the early days of television, producers and studios experimented with the new medium in ways that seem quaint today. Accustomed to radio techniques, news broadcasters simply read from a script while on camera. Comedy shows pointed a fixed camera or two at the actors standing by their microphones. Not everyone was accustomed to the presence of a camera—which created awkward and unintentionally hilarious results. (For examples of this today, look no further than YouTube ads featuring owners of small, local companies.)

Eventually, however, the nature and potential of the new medium became more familiar and better understood. Most people stopped trying to "do radio on TV" and stopped treating cameras as an awkward, uninvited presence.

The same phenomenon is true of virtual events today. We are familiar with live presentations, live meetings, and live classrooms. The physical presence of others in the room provides a familiar context—not to mention non-verbal feedback—that can make the event a success. However, the economic necessity of virtual events replaces people with their on-screen proxies.

We tend to overreact (or over-act) and let the distraction of technology keep us from making an effective online presentation, holding a successful meeting, or conducting a virtual class where people can actually learn.

To stop "doing radio on TV," virtual event facilitators need to embrace the new medium, accept its limitations, discover its advantages, and learn to play their old roles on a new stage.

COUNTERING PRECONCEPTIONS

The TV broadcasting mindset, while successful for news reporters and entertainers, is a liability for those conducting virtual events. Looking directly at the camera to "make eye contact," or reading a memorized script to convey an impression that the presenter or facilitator is somehow distant or aloof does not engage the audience. Even if you are a good actor, the sense that you're just playing a role lessens the impact of your content. For the vast majority of facilitators who are not good actors, the effect is even worse. A memorized script does not emotionally ring true and the feeling of being stared at is, at best, a distraction.

Instead, presenters and facilitators should largely ignore the camera and focus on the same material the audience sees—with frequent glances at different individuals' screens. When making a point, gestures and body language toward the camera—preferably natural and spontaneous—are perfectly fine. That comes more readily with experience.

Old TV habits die hard. Having a camera and lights in the room make many people overly nervous and self-conscious; it emboldens others to act unnaturally. Neither serves the objectives of a virtual meeting. Rather than attempting to become actors, virtual event leaders should always strive to make the technology a minor but necessary aspect of a normal, everyday process.

Another bad TV habit is the illusion that virtual events need to be polished and perfect. Most television shows are the result of painstaking preparation and editing by a small army of specialists. Even live broadcasts are carefully choreographed and rehearsed, and taped ones are thoroughly reconstructed before you see the finished product. Virtual events are not that. Even when there are no technical glitches (a truly rare occurrence), our humanity and its flaws are on full display throughout the event.

Presenters and facilitators can counter this delusion of perfection by simply ignoring the imperfections or making light of them. Whether the problem is technical or personal, the best course is to keep calm and carry on.

A third preconception comes not from a TV performance bias but from the scourge of live events: the presentation deck. As discussed in Chapter 2, a poor, text-heavy presentation does not fare better in a virtual event than it does in a live one. In fact, the results are usually worse. In a live event, viewers can experience "Death by PowerPoint" but by social convention and peer pressure are compelled to at least feign interest. In a virtual event, there are many more distractions and far fewer chances of being caught doing something else.

The skills of the virtual presenter or facilitator are far more important to the success of an event than are the technology itself. While a good technical producer is essential, it is the host who has learned to leverage the medium that makes the greatest impact.

BEST PRACTICES FOR VIRTUAL HOSTS

Virtual events, like live ones, always need a capable leader or host—someone who has the event objectives clearly in mind and has developed the skills necessary to get the group there. Some of these skills are simply extensions of what it takes to succeed in a live event, whereas others are unique to the virtual environment.

For all types of virtual events—information sessions, meetings, or trainings—the hosts physical setting is crucial. Everything that the other members see and hear, via a relatively narrow video window, affects how well or how poorly the information is received.

Personal Appearance – The role of a virtual event presenter, moderator, or facilitator is to maximize engagement, not attract attention. The object is to convey knowledge, not boost ratings (another TV-induced bias). Clothing and grooming standards vary among companies and organizations, but it is important to always convey respect and confidence—both ways—without creating undue distraction.

There are also technical considerations stemming from the nature of video, such as the dangers of wearing stripes that create a vibrating moiré pattern or becoming an unsettling "floating head" by wearing clothing the same color or shade as the background. Fortunately, a good technical producer can establish appropriate personal appearance guidelines for a virtual host in each type of event.

Lighting – Despite the fact many people are familiar with home cameras and smartphones, they still neglect the basic rules for lighting. Daylight is, of course, the best possible light source, but the vast majority of virtual events take place indoors. Ample windows can supply such light—provided they are *behind* the camera and *in front of* the subject, as to not create a backlit appearance.

Reliance on outdoor lighting is also problematic for other reasons, including time of day and outside weather conditions.

THE **VIRTUAL EVENTS PLAYBOOK**

For an event host in particular, the emphasis should always be on indoor lighting.

Depending on the frequency of events and their overall business importance, lighting for an event host can include a portable three-point lighting system. Ordinary room light often casts distracting shadows which makes the host difficult to see clearly. Overhead fluorescent lighting creates a blue cast, though this can be corrected by a competent technical producer.

A good rule for the virtual host or facilitator to follow is simply to preview themselves on camera. If the picture is good—and the producer agrees—then the lighting is acceptable. If not, then add lighting in front of the presenter and behind the camera at whatever angle produces the best-looking results.

The purpose of good lighting for the host is to provide clarity and eliminate distraction, not to make the host a star. While lighting for virtual participants is less important, lighting for the host is critical.

Sound – As with lighting, sound quality for the host is essential, to the point where redundant backups are mandatory.* For some types of virtual events, particularly meetings, video glitches can be borne so long as there is audio.

For the host, a high-quality, inconspicuous lapel mic is preferable, unless the presenter is already comfortable with a handheld or TED-style headset. For those speaking behind a desk or podium, a wired microphone is fine, but if he or she is a "rover," then a wireless, Lavalier-style device is essential. Sound quality (and price) varies with different devices, but remember that it is a business event, not a concert.

---

* A spare, pre-tested microphone is always a good idea. Any alternate option for voice communication—even an ordinary phone—minimizes the effects of Murphy's Law.

For presenters in a meeting—especially those involving more than one person in a room—a boundary microphone or a Polycom-style teleconferencing system is preferable—provided that people in the room can remain quiet.

Producers are in charge of monitoring sound levels before and during an event, but a host should be aware of the rules. Setting the sound level too high will pick up every distracting noise, including the hum of room lights, fans, and office equipment; setting it too low will make the speaker inaudible, which defeats the purpose of the entire event.

Finally, consider the acoustic properties of the room itself. While it is not necessary to achieve recording studio quality, the room used by a host should be relatively free of echoes and distracting sounds from outside sources (e.g., traffic, neighboring offices, or random pets and children).

"I CAN'T HEAR!"

Perhaps the most frequent text sent during any virtual event is that of a participant who can't hear the presenter. However, both the presenter and the producer should always remember that *one person complaining of audio issues does not mean everyone is having issues.*

The producer should always be monitoring audio to ensure that levels are correct. But very often the problem is a user issue that can be fixed with a prompt, direct response from the producer. Too often, a facilitator's first reaction to a "can't hear" message is to interrupt himself or herself and call everyone's attention to the technology. The problem is often as simple as a user muting their own headset—or another easily fixable issue. Unless it is a widespread, systemic issue (which is rare), the presenter should always leave such glitches in the producer's hands.

Background – It is usually pointless and often unnecessarily distracting to create an artificial "set" for a virtual event. What is appropriate for a television news or entertainment show is wholly counterproductive for an information session, meeting, or training venue. The same applies to using a green screen and swapping in an artificial background. The time, effort, and cost are wasted and the audience less apt to receive the information.

Instead, the background for a virtual event host should be simple and free from visual distractions. This includes excessive decorations or other visual clutter on the wall itself, but it could also include people walking or working behind the speaker. Even a blank or relatively blank wall is preferable to an "interesting" background containing distracting objects. The color should be relatively neutral and provide sufficient contrast for the host. For obvious reasons, it should not contain windows unless they can be completely curtained.

The Room Itself – A virtual event host should always be comfortable in the broadcast location, whether it's his or her regular office, an ad-hoc space, a boardroom or auditorium. This takes time and practice—all the more reason to leave the details of what camera to use and how to set everything up to a technical producer. However, there are some choices that the host should make beforehand.

If the host is more comfortable speaking from behind a desk or podium, then the room and its equipment should be arranged around it. However, if he or she is a "roamer," then a well-defined (and marked) space should be designated, with cameras positioned and controlled to cover it. Props of various kinds can be used, of course, but should be placed where they will not be a distraction. If a flip chart is to be used, it should be positioned—and a camera set to capture it—effectively. Certain visual aids, such as whiteboards, should be avoided if they create glare or other problems for video.

In short, the room used by the host, while not at the level of a broadcast studio, is still the physical "home" of the event. When the host is comfortable and at ease, the group members tend to be as well.

CONFESSIONS OF A ROVER

I am personally incapable of staying in one place while presenting to a virtual audience—or any audience, for that matter. So, as standard procedure when preparing for virtual events, my producer and I put tape down, marking the areas of the floor where I will be fully on camera. Since most virtual events do not involve a moveable camera, this is a wise precaution for most presenters that share my aversion to speaking from a fixed position.

Another important lesson comes from my habit of using a flip chart whenever I speak. (My colleagues make bets on how soon I will leap toward a flip chart if one is in the room.) Making sure that a flip chart is within the taped-off boundaries of a "rover's" territory is essential to the success of a presentation. It's also a good idea to have a second camera focused on the flip chart itself—with room for the speaker on one side or the other—so that the producer can switch from the main camera to a close-up of the chart whenever it's appropriate.

Attitude, Attitude, Attitude – A good virtual event host must not only unlearn preconceptions about "being on TV," he or she must also learn how to enjoy the new medium. It helps if they already enjoy live events, but the key to success in either venue is to view presentation, meeting facilitation, or training as positive activities—or even fun ones.

For virtual events, the first and often hardest step is to not dwell on the technology itself, either the positive, fascinating aspects or the frustrating ones. Most virtual event platforms have intriguing, innovative features, but an experienced host should spend little or no time marveling about them. Likewise, when technical problems occur, no useful purpose is served by dwelling on them. The adage, "Keep Calm, and Carry On," should be the mantra of every virtual presenter, facilitator, and trainer. With the help of a competent technical producer behind the scenes, the host can do so—and focus on the purpose of the event.

Finally, the nature of virtual events opens new possibilities for hosts that are not possible with live events. Participants with different learning styles or emotional makeups might be less likely to speak up in a live meeting but more likely to participate in a virtual one. This is due in part to tools that allow for less conspicuous, or even anonymous contribution. Extroverts and verbal learners will still be noticed, but the virtual playing field potentially provides more opportunity for participation from more reserved learners.

With that in mind, a virtual facilitator can listen more broadly, encourage better ideas, and achieve better results—if they are willing to learn from the new environment.

PARTICIPANT BEST PRACTICES

Marketing guru Geoffrey Moore divided technology adopters into distinct categories. On one end, the innovators and early adopters (visionaries) tend to show boundless enthusiasm for any new technology and embrace it, despite its flaws. Pragmatists and conservatives—whom Moore described as early and late majority adopters, respectively—require proof of concept and successful adoption by others before they too can embrace the change. Laggards, as one might expect, are highly skeptical, constantly finding fault with technology and adopting it only under protest.

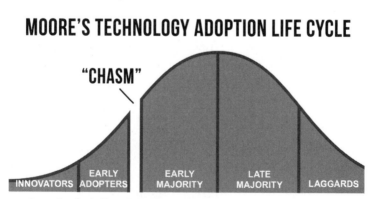

MOORE'S TECHNOLOGY ADOPTION LIFE CYCLE

Source: *Crossing the Chasm*, Harper Business Essentials, Copyright ©1991 by Geoffrey Moore

Moore's description is apt for virtual event platforms—not only for the companies who buy them, but the individuals who are asked to use them. On the visionary end, users jump in right away. They probably over-use a platform's tools and possibly miss the overall point of the event. On the skeptical end, users balk at the slightest provocation, and potentially stampede others into resisting the process. Part of the event facilitator's job is to manage these two extremes, but his or her most important "selling" task is to persuade the majority and enlist their support.

The best way to establish proof of concept to a majority of users is to have a clear set of best practices for ordinary members in a virtual event and to highlight successful examples when they occur. Whenever an average user (not an enthusiast) makes good use of the technology to further the event's objectives, the host should make that clear to the group. This does not mean stopping to praise a particular user. Rather, it should be more subtle, like noticing something relevant or interesting in the user's location. It could also be a pointed response to a non-verbal cue, such as, "Joanne, it looks like you have something to say here," or "Max, you seem puzzled." By using the technology to make a virtual event more like a live one, the host can show the majority of users that it is normal and beneficial.

Every virtual event has unique user requirements, but there are some universal best practices:

Physical Environment – Each participant in an event broadcasts from their own personal space, whether it's an actual office, a home office, or (in many cases) a bedroom or hotel room. This means that any expectations of "studio conditions" must be banished from the start. Visually distracting clutter in the background is unavoidable in most cases, but the user can take reasonable steps to minimize it. As a practical step, when doing a camera check, ask each user to turn around and "see what the camera sees." Most users will spot the obvious or potentially embarrassing background distractions and move them before the meeting begins.

Unlike the presenter or facilitator, a regular participant does not need to have a blank wall as a background. In fact, the presence of interesting (but not too distracting) objects or furnishings can be a part of that person's on-screen persona. Rather than trying to control the space of each user, a good facilitator uses it to the meeting's advantage.

Finally, there is always the potential for embarrassing or distracting intrusions into the user's physical environment by pets, children, and significant others. Some can be minimized by finding an area that doesn't include shared spaces; for example, by not having a bathroom in the camera's field of view. Despite precautions, however, incidents invariably occur. When they do, an astute producer will be prepared to cut a camera feed and address the problem in a private chat or text. Obviously, the unpredictable nature of virtual events requires tolerance and a good sense of humor.

Lighting – While a room's physical appearance can be left to a user's discretion, the correct use of light is more demanding. No user should be required to purchase studio lighting, but every user should follow some basic rules:

- *Never have a window at your back* unless you can draw the curtain or close the blinds. The "witness protection" look is not a good one for any team member.

- *Never use your monitor as a primary light source.* The "scary hacker" look is also not ideal.

- *Make sure there are more lights in front of you than behind or above you.* Although studio lighting is not a practical option, having more than one light source on your face usually creates a normal appearance.

- *Warmer is better.* Fluorescent lighting and some LED bulbs create a decidedly cool appearance. Incandescent bulbs tend to appear warmer. If you have a choice, go with the latter.

Sound – The quality of a personal computer or tablet microphone is totally outside the control of a virtual event leader or producer. While a headset with a built-in microphone is preferable to using a device's speakers, it is usually not reasonable to insist that a participant buy special audio equipment. (Fortunately, most smartphones now include suitable ear plugs with a built-in microphone, allowing users to participate via teleconference.) Variances in sound quality can be managed by performing an informal sound check at the beginning of the event, and by asking the producer to assist users with adjusting the volume directly. Many "sound problems" can be traced to user actions, such as inadvertently muting their headset or clicking the mute button in the software. In such cases, a producer's assistance—preferably in private chats—is invaluable.

Camera – Like microphones and speakers, webcams are not reliably consistent across users. However, the point of a virtual meeting is *not* to emulate a remote TV broadcast. Variations in image resolution should not be viewed as a flaw in the system. So long as each user is clearly visible, in a well-lit room relatively clear of avoidable distractions, then the focus should be on the event.

THE MASTER PLAN

Every successful virtual event should be preceded by a thorough planning process. If the event is informational in nature, the "master plan" should encompass not only the presentation deck (preferably a concise one), but also the agenda of individual speakers and subject matter experts. The number of slides to use is a critical calculation. If an hour-long session, not counting Q&A, contains over thirty slides, and each of these requires significant time to discuss—or worse, read aloud—then the event will invariably fail.

Planning an information session for one speaker or many requires expert organization and rehearsal. Although such an event is not strictly a performance, it should be managed with strict time limits in mind. The presenter or facilitator should always know the key takeaways for each segment and build the discussion and examples accordingly—knowing what can be cut, if necessary.

A key element of the plan is knowing how to use virtual event tools—and when to refrain from using them. Used discreetly, these can keep the audience engaged in a one-way video environment. When over-used, they can distract and annoy. Poll questions should be used sparingly, no more than four or five in a one-hour event. Other community engagement tools, such as emoticons and chat, should be handled solely by the producer, not the host or other speakers. Similarly, submitted text questions should be curated during the event, used during the Q&A portion, and later transcribed in a post-event FAQ.

Participant involvement is the key to any session. There are many techniques for engaging participation, starting with asking for questions or volunteers—either spontaneously during the session or by seeding the questions beforehand. Participants can be contacted privately—before the session begins—and asked to submit questions or be prepared to respond on a particular topic. Seeded questions not only add value to the presentation, they can also "prime the pump," cueing others in the group to engage.

Another common technique, commonly referred to as *voluntold*, is used when you choose a participant who has not volunteered. Whether you are not getting any volunteers from the audience members or the same two or three people keep raising their hands, you can voluntold someone who is not participating very much. Keep in mind, however, that some people simply need time to collect their thoughts before they provide an answer, so don't always pick the first volunteer—or assume that the quiet participant is not engaged.

Planning a meeting or training is less about the presentation and more about the event objectives. Specific business goals or knowledge can be overtly stated or implicit, but they must clearly exist and be measurable in some manner. If the event is freeform in nature, such as a brainstorming session, the measurable objective may simply be an organized plan of action. If the event involves specific knowledge or skill levels, then each learning objective must have a related, measurable outcome, such as increased sales or customer service successes.

Of course, no plan survives the battle. Invariably, through technical issues or non-technical distractions, a virtual event can go off course and produce less than satisfactory results. Diminishing undesirable factors is partly achieved by choosing the right platform and following the guidelines in this book. But when the inevitable occurs, a proactive host and producer team use that unfortunate experience to build a better one.

RISK MANAGEMENT 101

When we first started our virtual event business, we made several assumptions that were correct *in theory* but vulnerable to the effects of Murphy's Law. We evaluated several different platforms—as we continue to do—and selected the appropriate one for each situation. So far, so good.

For one particularly complex training event, we based our platform choice on several factors, the most important of which was high-quality video. The platform also had to have a full set of training-specific features. We made our selection and proceeded on the assumption that this platform would be used for *everything*—video, audio, community engagement, and individual engagement.

On the day of the event, the platform crashed—spectacularly. Users still had a video feed from the instructor but nothing else. We managed to send the trainees a message by writing on a flipchart and holding it up to the camera. Eventually, we managed to reset, restart, and complete the event, but it was not our finest hour.

Our first takeaway from that fiasco has since become a cardinal rule for our company:

In low-latency situations, where interaction takes precedence over video quality, ALWAYS separate the audio and video components of a virtual event.

This means using teleconferencing for the audio portion of an event rather than using computer audio or VOIP. Even though all platforms support using computer audio, and encourage people to do so, it creates an unacceptable and avoidable risk. Ordinary teleconferencing is extremely reliable and can be enhanced with a decent headset. If any aspect of the platform fails, users will at least have a phone link to the event.

This is not a strict rule with high-latency, livestreamed events. These involve video resolutions of 4K or higher, and typically do not include two-way interaction, simply because the lagtime is too high. However, when effectively managed, livestreamed events can include computer audio *and* video with far less overall risk.

———

Another important lesson learned from this event and others is the necessity of a backup strategy. Very recently, we experienced a platform server crash in the middle of a virtual training event. Although it only affected four out of twenty-five virtual "rooms" that day, the failure was complete. But this time, we were prepared.

Before the event had begun, we had designated a backup platform and had uploaded the training presentation to it as a precaution. When the server crash occurred, we immediately notified all the participants, instructing them to log in to the backup platform. Performance was noticeably slower, and users did not have access to the same interactivity features, but the learning objectives were accomplished.

Obviously, it is not cost-effective to prepare a complete duplicate program on two separate platforms, on the chance the preferred platform fails. However, being *ready* to switch to an alternate platform is essential. Besides having an available platform account, you must decide what constitutes a "Minimum Viable Presentation," or MVP. This is usually a PowerPoint or PDF that can be uploaded quickly to the backup platform. Other features, especially those based on specific platform features, may need to be ignored.

In the final analysis, a good risk management strategy must give your producer the power to make one of three choices following a platform failure:

1. **Should we (and can we) instruct participants to log out and log back in?**

2. **Should we have them log out and switch to the backup platform, after the MVP is uploaded and ready? This goes with the assumption that the experience will be different and not as full-featured, but still adequate.**

3. **Should we simply reschedule the event?**

Each of these choices is less than ideal, but being prepared to make them is a crucial requirement for any virtual event.

PULL-THROUGH STRATEGIES

Virtual knowledge transfer, like its live counterpart, is often "push" oriented—top-down, management-driven, and relatively static. Participants are required to digest whatever comes their way, prove they comprehend it to some degree, and are (hopefully) given opportunities to apply it. It can also be "pull" oriented—learner-driven, collaborative, dynamic, and available when it is most needed.

Both approaches have a valid place in business, and both can be facilitated by the use of virtual technology. A well-run information session can provide measured amounts of "push" content, while virtual meetings and trainings can combine both "push" and "pull" through user interaction, breakout sessions, and teach-backs.

The timing of multiple sessions is vital when creating a pull-through strategy. Following an initial information session, a 30-day, 60-day, and 90-day series of meetings allows the participants to put the new information into practice, discuss the results, and explore expanded or alternative courses of action. Facilitators should be prepared to alter their core information session as a result—or plan new events based on the experience.

Trainings should also follow the 30-60-90 approach to pull-through. Verbal fluency skills learned in a single event only improve with repetition and examination of the results. Conducting follow-up trainings based on these experiences reinforces the learning and provides the opportunity for participants to generate their own best practices.

Virtual events—like their live counterparts—succeed or fail based on the strengths and preparedness of the host or presenter. Although choosing the right platform and a capable producer are important, it is ultimately the host's personal connection with the audience that is the determining factor. Mastering the realities of virtual event technology is a learnable skill that often builds on existing strengths and abilities. While not every presenter, facilitator, or trainer will successfully make the jump to virtual events, those who do succeed are likely those who already have the people skills that have always made events successful.

■ ■ ■

CHAPTER SUMMARY

Always remember that virtual, online, video-enabled events are not the equivalent of news or entertainment broadcasting. Presenters and participants in virtual events should not feel or act like they're "on TV."

A virtual event host or presenter should always use a high-quality (1080p) camera, a lapel microphone or headset, sufficient lighting, and a simple, non-distracting background.

A virtual event participant can have a lower-resolution camera but should always use a headset—preferably with his or her phone, not VOIP—to reduce ambient noise. Lighting is important but not as crucial as for a presenter or facilitator. The background need not be empty but should have minimal clutter.

Before a session begins, always check behind you to make sure your background is free from distracting or potentially embarrassing elements. Also, if possible, close and lock doors through which partners, children, or pets may unexpectedly intrude.

Wherever possible, have a planned objective for every virtual event, and for its related follow-up or "pull-through" events.

Active Content

To access the free, active content resources for this chapter, use your mobile device to scan the chapter's QR Code, below, or type in the URL provided.

https://letstrainonline.com/ch5

THE **VIRTUAL EVENTS PLAYBOOK**

CHAPTER SIX

Planning for a Crisis

I n early 2020, the world faced an unprecedented business and social challenge imposed by the COVID-19 pandemic. Public health measures to contain the spread of the virus included social distancing and stay-at-home mandates, which required working from home wherever possible. Almost overnight, individuals and businesses had to make the shift and rely on the technologies and methods described in this book for company-wide information sessions, regular meetings, and trainings.

Not everyone was successful. For the most part, the internet itself handled the increased load, as it was designed to do. However, many organizations and employees struggled with the sudden transition. Lack of familiarity with platforms and their strengths and weaknesses, combined with normal at-home distractions and an overall lack of preparedness, led to less than ideal results for some.

This chapter is not a shortcut to rapid deployment of a virtual event strategy. Going virtual requires planning, support, and a thorough knowledge of the platforms and their capabilities.

However, while there is no way to undo the past, this chapter may serve as a guide to using virtual events during the next crisis—as well as under normal conditions.

A TALE OF TWO COMPANIES

When the COVID-19 pandemic hit, we worked with two U.S. companies attempting a rapid shift to virtual events. One had over two years of experience using virtual event technology and had a dedicated producer who oversaw roughly forty-six events per year. The other company used the same platform (Adobe Connect) for some events, but their team had only basic familiarity with its capabilities. For smaller meetings, they used a different platform with moderate success.

When the work-from-home mandate hit, the first company had procedures in place, as well as dedicated resources with full knowledge of the platform. In relatively short order, they scaled up to 238 events. Executives and other team leaders were able to facilitate their events from home with just modest environmental upgrades in lighting, backgrounds, and recording equipment.

The other company initially insisted on using live-streaming for major events, followed by contiguous breakout sessions for smaller groups. However, their virtual events had to be significantly scaled back due to the fact that the original venue for broadcasting was closed and because smaller groups were not used to Adobe Connect for regular meetings. They discovered that large virtual events required more planning time than they could afford to spend.

Both companies survived the debacle, but only the first one did so without losing the full benefits of virtual engagement and interaction.

THE CRISIS MVP

Software developers typically rely on a milestone known as the Minimum Viable Product (MVP)—that combination of absolutely essential features without which the software cannot be released to the public. Similarly, companies and organizations facing the need to rely suddenly and exclusively on virtual event technology must also prepare their own MVP. Eventually, they can (and should) add the "nice to have" capabilities that virtual events provide. Many of these are described elsewhere in this book and in its online "active content." But for the short term, here are the basics:

Network Connectivity – The most obvious requirement is internet access. For event leaders and facilitators, this must involve a robust broadband connection. Fortunately, such connections are becoming commonplace. For participants, a slower connection, such as DSL or a mobile hotspot, is acceptable, provided the group is aware of the potential for latency and occasional disconnects.

Platform – Any of the virtual event platforms listed in Chapter 1 (and in the book's online content) will be sufficient. However, the platform must be carefully chosen, not only for its features but also for scalability (depending on company and meeting size), stability, security, and support. Also, at least one company member must become *thoroughly* familiar with the chosen platform and its capabilities. This is necessary not only to provide support but also to plan and define the scope of typical virtual meetings.

Separate Audio and Video – As a general rule, always use dial-in teleconferencing (as opposed to computer audio) when participating in a virtual event. While VOIP is a convenient, standard feature on all platforms, relying on internet connectivity for *everything* can be a source of problems. If a participant's internet connection fails during a meeting, their audio participation will continue.

Backup Materials – For any virtual event, it is always wise to have a backup copy of the documents, presentations, and shared screens being used. This is especially important for the team leader or facilitator, who must be able to continue the meeting when connectivity is interrupted. It is not necessary (or even advisable) for participants to have such materials in advance, as they tend to distract from the conversation. However, an emergency DropBox or other cloud storage link is a useful backup strategy in the event that the visual connection is lost.

Patience, Forbearance, and a Sense of Humor – Even under ideal conditions, technical glitches and awkward moments are (and probably always will be) the hallmark of virtual events. During crisis conditions, these qualities are even more essential.

If a crisis is prolonged, the MVP can be built upon, adding best practices and procedures for presenters and participants, as described elsewhere in the book. However, these essentials allow you to not only survive a stay-at-home situation, but possibly even enjoy it.

A TIERED APPROACH

Under normal conditions, larger events, including information sessions and webinars, typically involve one-way video communication with limited interaction (e.g., polls and emoticons) with the audience. This can be accomplished via low-latency platforms, albeit with lower video resolution than high-latency live-streaming. (See Chapter 3 sidebar, "Latency and Resolution.") Some platforms also allow large events to split up into simultaneous breakout sessions for greater person-to-person interaction.

In a crisis, however, it is far more difficult to hold such a complex virtual event. If the actual building used for broadcasting is closed, then live-streaming is almost certainly excluded, as are many studio-like scenarios used by low-latency platforms. When the speaker or facilitator is also home-bound, the virtual event workflow must change.

Typically, this means that larger events must be broken down into sessions and even held over several days instead of all at once. A main session can be conducted on a low-latency platform—preferably with good lighting, background, and video. But the breakout sessions usually cannot be held simultaneously—or even on the same day as the main session.

As with everything attempted during a crisis, expectations for virtual events must be set appropriately. Doing without the "glitz and glam" of a high-end presentation enables effective large events.

ASKING FOR HELP

Virtual events, especially those involving large audiences and complex training or learning objectives, cannot be done casually, even under normal circumstances. Nominal familiarity with platforms is no substitute for thoughtful planning and production expertise. This is especially true under crisis conditions.

The first course of action when it comes to expertise is to develop outside resources. Whether or not you hire an experienced producer, you need to have access to experts in your platform of choice. However, in normal times as well as during a crisis, the success of your virtual events depends on your willingness to reach out to (and compensate) those who can sustain your virtual event strategy.

More importantly, everyone planning a virtual event contingency must develop at least one person internally who understands the chosen platform. The number of needed experts varies depending on the size of your company or organization. However, their knowledge of virtual event capabilities ensures success in a crisis and over the long term.

THE PLANNING PROCESS

Before a crisis occurs, there are several basic steps every business or organization should take to ensure their readiness. Many are elaborated elsewhere in the book, but here are the essentials:

Establish a Standard Environment – For speakers and meeting facilitators, this means making sure each person's location (in the office and at home) is optimized for video and audio quality. This includes lighting conditions, suitable cameras and microphones, a robust internet connection, and a suitable, non-distracting background.* For attendees, this also means

---

* Some platforms offer artificial, digitally-created backgrounds for videoconferencing. While these may seem appealing, they add to internet traffic overhead, making connection continuity less certain. A better alternative is to use a physical pop-up background or simply an attractive, well-lit area of the room.

suitable lighting and environmental conditions, although typically less stringent than those of a presenter.

Testing and Rehearsal – The best time to deal with any crisis is before it happens. For virtual events, this means testing new platform components, evaluating them during normal conditions, and documenting best practices. For every major virtual event, even under crisis conditions, the importance of rehearsal cannot be underestimated. The speaker must not only be comfortable with the subject matter, but also prepared to handle the opportunities and challenges of the virtual medium.

Support Contingencies – Under normal conditions, a production support person or team should be prepared to handle inevitable glitches and interruptions. The facilitator should never call attention to these—and with a good production team, should never have to. Such issues are more common during crisis conditions, so the technical producers should amass as much experience as possible in dealing with this unpredictable medium.

Planning for a possible crisis should not be significantly different from virtual event planning in general. Setting expectations, allowing sufficient time to establish learning and event goals, and creating best practices are just as useful in a crisis as they are during the normal course of business.

FROM MVP TO SOP

Virtual event technology is relatively new and changing rapidly. Many companies have not yet had the time or inclination to create standard operating procedures for virtual information sessions, meetings, or trainings. (Hopefully, this book will help fill that gap.) However, there's nothing quite like a pandemic or other crisis to spur action.

Whether we are preparing for the next traumatic event or thinking about long-term business goals, virtual event technology is a permanent part of business communication. Hopefully, the process of building lifeboats leads us to building better vessels to support our larger business goals.

■ ■ ■

CHAPTER SUMMARY

In a crisis environment, the "Minimum Viable Product" for virtual events includes basic network connectivity, a single, suitable platform, separate audio and video usage, a strategy for backup materials, and a sense of humor and proportion.

The luxuries of simultaneous high-end presentation and interaction must always take second place to utility and practicality.

Expertise and planning are indispensable during a crisis and invaluable after the crisis has passed. Ideally, the virtual event practices we develop for future crises will serve us equally well as standard operating procedures.

Active Content

To access the free, active content resources for this chapter, use your mobile device to scan the chapter's QR Code, below, or type in the URL provided.

https://letstrainonline.com/ch6

EPILOGUE

Taking the Plunge

Since you've taken the time to read this book, you clearly want to improve your virtual facilitation skills. You may already be a seasoned in-person presenter, facilitator, or trainer—with natural abilities to connect with an audience. You may excel at one-on-one interaction but less certain about working with large groups—in-person or online. Whether you're a veteran or a rookie, however, you're probably uncomfortable with the idea of jumping into virtual events.

This is completely natural. Adopting a new perspective—or changing an existing one—is always difficult, especially if you've had a bad first* experience with online events. Your experiences shape your beliefs, so, if you are going to change your beliefs about virtual events, you must be open to new experiences. This means, initially, working outside your comfort zone. In time and with the techniques outlined in this book, handling a virtual meeting will feel as normal as driving a car. Despite your reservations now, you will be able to accomplish the same objectives in the virtual environment as you are in person.

---

* Or second. Or third.

The first step to becoming an outstanding virtual facilitator is to unlearn a very common misconception—that anything virtual is inherently inferior. In fact, virtual is simply a *different* approach to an age-old problem: conveying information to those who need it. Don't get me wrong: if you have the budget and can afford the participants' time away from their jobs long enough to attend an in-person event, then live training can be amazingly effective. But you picked up this book because you have a reason for conducting your events virtually. Whether reduced budgets or because the extra time and travel would impair participants' ability to be in front of customers, you need to master this unfamiliar medium and become a better virtual facilitator.

When I first started virtual training in the wake of an unexpected travel ban, I wanted nothing to do with it. I told myself it would only last until the ban was lifted; afterward, I would be back to training in person. At first, this plan went as expected. We completed the first new hire training virtually, the travel ban was lifted, and we went back to in-person training. But—there is always a "but" in these stories—the virtual element did not go away.

We began to add online components to the pre-training, home study cycles. Participants came into the live training more prepared than before, which shortened the new hire training time by twenty-five percent. Then, as sometimes happens, we had a large reorganization training, this time for over 400 sales representatives. The budget was insufficient to support everyone traveling to a single location for the training. To make matters worse, it was in December—just before the holidays, not the most popular time for extra travel. Virtual training was the obvious alternative.

Fortunately by this point, our virtual techniques had improved. We had great two-way audio and video communication, as well as small group sessions with breakouts. To everyone's satisfaction, the participants were meeting the same objectives we had for in-person training.

Participant feedback was better than we had expected. Of course, not having to travel in December made participants happy. (One of the iconic photos from the reorganization training was a participant with the Christmas tree in the background.) But beyond that, everyone passed their certifications, and all survey results showed they felt prepared to go into the field to sell to customers. Despite my preconceptions, virtual really worked. If I had clung to my old beliefs, it would have been a "one and done" expedient. But fortunately, I had a director who pushed me outside of my comfort zone to become a virtual facilitator.

Another important step is recognizing that being a virtual event leader is not the same as being a broadcaster or an entertainer. Being uncomfortable or camera-shy is perfectly natural. Most people don't like how they look or sound on camera, and that feeling is aggravated by thinking of it as a stage performance. It's not. You won't be perfect the first time—or even the twenty-first time—you facilitate a virtual event, but perfection is not the point. You become accustomed, even comfortable leading a virtual event, just as you were with live ones. It gets better with practice and familiarity.

An especially important step is recognizing that technology—however new—is not the enemy. Glitches happen, but calling attention to them only slows you down and prevents your team from benefitting fully. With a good technical producer or assistant, nearly all technology problems can be avoided or mitigated—giving you the freedom to become a great facilitator.

There are two main goals we hoped to accomplish with this book: first, to provide many ideas on how virtual events can be implemented to accomplish the desired objectives. By going beyond the stereotypical webinar model (also known as "Death by PowerPoint"), these objective techniques can help make your small group training sessions just as engaging as your in-person events.

Second, we hope illustrating our experiences helps you alter the belief that all virtual events are inferior to in-person ones. It can be the exact opposite. There are instances when you can be even more interactive and engaging virtually than in person.

After reading this book, the challenge is to change your perspective about virtual events. So, when planning your first virtual event, always follow these steps:

1. Determine the objectives of the event.

2. Find the virtual event platform that accomplishes your objectives.

3. Design the event engagement based on the objectives.

Not surprisingly, all three steps are comparable to those preceding a live event. You are merely substituting some different tools and techniques to build a great learning experience.

If you change the way you think about your events from the start, the effectiveness of your events will increase dramatically, and you will find new and more creative ways to implement virtual events. Some of these you will be able to accomplish on your own. Some may require a virtual event production team. All will help you become a great virtual facilitator.

The biggest winners of all are your participants. Using these tools and techniques, you will be able to train them at a higher level than your resources and time previously allowed—and help them succeed together.

ACKNOWLEDGMENTS

There are a few people we'd like to thank for their influence when this all began. First, to Mike Capaldi, our former Vice President of Training, who was willing to let us find a solution to the travel restrictions imposed by the Swine Flu. We'd also like to thank Jeff Taylor, who was Stanley and Lee's Senior Director at the time. He pushed us outside our comfort zone even when we pushed back and believed we could develop an effective virtual training event with a short timeline. He also made sure we had the resources needed to improve the learner experience.

Tony Busa, our manager, provided encouragement and asked the questions we needed to answer as we developed the solution. He provided positive encouragement and made sure we continued to look forward when negativity started to enter into our first virtual sessions. He also helped us analyze the situation, make adjustments, and find ways to improve the training.

Finally, when the rubber met the road and we all had to implement our plans, we couldn't have asked for a better group of trainers to figure this all out with. Thanks to Michael Donovan, Shane Gorman, Scott McConnell, Justin Mott, Charity Patrick, and Todd Miller. From the time the first message came down (that we had to train forty representatives on three products in less than a week—virtually) until launch, everyone helped each other out. We all sat in our cubes and figured out how we could use Adobe Connect Pro to effectively train participants. Then, we had nightly debriefings on how to improve training. Throughout, we made frequent shopping trips to get cameras, lights, and the required cords and cables to live-stream a camcorder through a computer—over ten long years ago.

A lot has changed with the technology over the years since that first event, but we kept learning as a group for the next eighteen months. A lot of those principles that we learned together are now a major part of this book. Thank you to everyone for all you did to contribute to the success of our learners. We could not have asked for a better group of people so willing to share their successes for the betterment of the team—and ultimately, for the representatives who sat at the computers on the other side.